Africa's Greatest
Explorer

To our grandkids:
Devin, Woods, Jack, Charlotte, Ben
with a grandpa's earnest prayers
for your saving faith in Jesus Christ
and your loving service of him.

Africa's Greatest Explorer

David Livingstone

Vance Christie

CF4·K

10 9 8 7 6 5 4 3 2 1

Copyright © 2024 Vance Christie
Paperback ISBN: 978-1-5271-1163-9
Ebook ISBN: 978-1-5271-1203-2

Published by Christian Focus Publications,
Geanies House, Fearn, Tain, Ross-shire,
IV20 1TW, Scotland, U.K.
www.christianfocus.com
email: info@christianfocus.com

Cover design by Daniel van Straaten
Cover illustration by Graham Kennedy
Printed and bound by Nørhaven, Denmark

Contents

Cotton Mill Work and Night School Studies

'David, it's time to wake up and get ready for work.'

Ten-year-old David Livingstone heard his mother's quiet voice and felt her gently shaking his shoulder to help awaken him. Opening his eyes, he saw her smiling down. His brother John, two years older than he, was already sitting up, rubbing the sleep from his eyes.

'Alright, Mother,' David said as he slowly sat up. He felt tired after doing school homework till late the previous evening and not getting a full night of rest. But he knew he needed to get up right away, in order to be at the cotton factory where John and he worked by 6 a.m.

'Shhhhh!' Agnes Livingstone reminded her two oldest sons in a whisper as they got up. 'Don't wake the wee ones. They're still sleeping.' David glanced over at his three younger siblings – Janet and Charles, ages five and two, and Agnes the baby.

The Livingstone family lived in a tiny one-room apartment that was only fourteen feet long and ten feet wide. A small wood-burning cook stove, which also provided heat for the apartment, was nestled under a mantel at one end of the room. The only furnishings in the room were a smallish table, a few wooden chairs of different sizes, and a chest of drawers. The apartment also had two little side nooks, each with a bed, where family members slept. Some of the children also slept on the floor. This had been David's only home from birth.

'Good morning, lads,' David and John's father, Neil Livingstone, greeted them pleasantly as they started getting dressed.

'Good morning, Father,' they responded.

As was the case many early mornings, Mr Livingstone was sitting at the table reading his Bible by the light of a candle and enjoying a hot cup of tea. Another candle glowed on the mantel above the stove.

Neil Livingstone was a traveling tea salesman. People appreciated his honesty, kindness and friendliness. While selling tea Mr Livingstone also passed out Gospel tracts, which told people about the Good News of salvation through faith in Christ Jesus.

Mr Livingstone was a dedicated Christian and worked hard at his business. However, he had a difficult time earning enough money to provide food, clothes, housing, and the other material needs of his family. That is why the Livingstones lived in such a tiny apartment with so few possessions. That is also why David and John, though only ten and twelve years old, needed to work in the local cotton factory to help provide money for their family.

Many families in Scotland and other parts of Britain during the 1820s were poor like the Livingstones. Back then there were few good-paying jobs available, so many people had to work long hours for a small amount of pay. In those days most boys received only a grammar school education and were expected, beginning at quite a young age, to get a job and learn a trade to help support their family.

Twenty-four families lived in the three-story brick tenement building where the Livingstones resided. Each family had only a small apartment like the Livingstones' with no indoor plumbing, so families had to carry water to their homes in a bucket. Bathing and toilet facilities, which were shared with the other families, were located near the tenement building.

Before David and John left their home that morning, Mrs Livingstone gave them a quick inspection, as she did nearly every day. 'My goodness, David,' she said when she saw that his coat sleeves did not reach to his wrists, 'you're growing so quickly you'll soon be too big for this jacket.' She used her fingers to brush aside an unruly strand of dark brown hair that fell across David's forehead above his hazel-colored eyes. 'And what are we going to do about this shaggy hair of yours? You're past due for a haircut.'

David smiled up at his mother but quickly ducked away from her grooming hands. She always worked so hard, caring for her family and keeping their small home neat and tidy. There never seemed to be any end to all the work she needed to do – cleaning and sweeping the house, cooking and baking food, washing dishes and laundry, as well as sewing and mending clothes.

Mrs Livingstone loved, encouraged and supported her husband and children. She promoted a positive, peaceful and cheery spirit in their home. She never complained about her heavy workload or the fact that their family had so little money or other possessions. But she could not always hide the worries she sometimes had because of their constant short supply of money.

It was only a short walk from the tenement building to the large cotton mill in their small town of Blantyre, Scotland, population 2,000 and just eight miles from the large city of Glasgow. The Blantyre cotton mill was a long, tall rectangular building that overlooked the banks of the River Clyde. The mill was built of bricks and had been painted white. Scores of large windows, stacked five stories high, lined its sides.

Inside the mill, rows of large cotton-spinning machines filled the factory's big open rooms. Those machines spun the cotton into yarn or thread. The factory was terribly noisy when the machines, with their many moving parts, were running and people were shouting above the sound of the machinery. The inside of the mill was also very hot. The factory was steam-heated to between eighty and ninety degrees Fahrenheit because hot, moist conditions were needed to make good quality thread.

David worked as a piecer at the mill. His job was to piece together threads on the spinning frames that were fraying or had broken. With as many as 100 lines of thread being used on a single spinning machine, he had many threads to watch carefully. In addition to needing sharp eyes, he also had to be agile because much of his work was done while balancing over the machine or crawling under its many lines of thread.

Several hundred people worked at the cotton mill. More than one-quarter of that number were teenagers or children as young as nine years of age. Even young children like David often worked twelve hours a day and around seventy hours per week! Mill employees commonly worked from 6 a.m. till 8 p.m., six days a week. David was always glad when it was time for their half-hour breakfast break and their hour-long lunch break.

The company that owned the mill also operated an evening school for its youth employees. The school met from 8 to 10 p.m. When David's long, tiring workday was finished, he went straight to school for two hours rather than going home to rest. Many young people who worked at the factory did not have the interest or energy to attend school after their wearisome workdays.

However, David loved learning and had a strong desire to get a good education. During his younger years he had learned 'the three R's' (reading, writing and arithmetic) in a small school that met in a lower room of the tenement building where his family lived.

Now that he had started working, he was determined to continue his education. His parents encouraged and supported him in doing so.

The year before, when he was nine years old, David had shown his sharp mind and diligent spirit in a Bible memory challenge from his Sunday School teacher at the Old Parish Church in Blantyre. David memorized all 176 verses of Psalm 119, which is the longest chapter in the Bible. He recited the entire psalm to his teacher with only five errors. As a reward for his outstanding accomplishment, he received a New Testament.

One of the subjects that David started studying during his first year at the evening school was Latin. 'If you want a good education,' his teacher William McSkimming told him kindly, 'then you must study Latin. Latin is the language of great men of learning.' David continued to study Latin with Mr McSkimming's help for several years. He learned it well and was able to read the writings of famous ancient Roman poets like Virgil and Horace.

David always clearly remembered the night when he returned home with his wages from his first long week of work at the mill. After entering their family apartment, he excitedly crossed the room to where his mother was sitting. He proudly placed the very first half-crown piece that he had earned in her lap. It was worth two shillings and six pence or one-eighth of a pound. 'Here, Mother,' he stated, 'now you won't need to worry so much about needing money.' When her eyes clouded with tears, he added: 'Don't cry, Mother. I want you to be happy.'

'I am happy, David,' she said as a smile came to her lips. 'These are tears of joy. I'm so thankful for you and John helping us out like this, and rightly proud of both of you.'

'I'm proud of you boys also,' David's father added. Then, knowing his son had received a few pence more than half a crown for his first week's wages, Mr Livingstone asked: 'What are you going to do with the rest of your earnings?'

'I'm going to buy a copy of Ruddiman's *Rudiments of Latin*,' David answered definitely. That was a grammar book that would help him learn Latin. He did indeed buy that book and wore it out using it. In the years that followed he continued to give most of his earnings from work to help provide money for his family.

When David arrived home after his shift at the mill and two hours of night school, he still needed to do his school homework. Even though he was tired, he pushed himself to complete it. As he grew older and his homework became more difficult, he often studied till midnight or later. Sometimes his mother got out of bed and took his books from his hands, stating: 'You must go to bed now, son.'

'But, Mother …,' he would begin to protest.

'No buts,' she would say firmly. 'You have to be back at the mill by six o'clock in the morning. You're not going to get enough rest as it is.'

13

David loved to read. Books about science and people's travels were his favorites. He had no interest in reading novels. And much to his father's disappointment and concern, he showed little interest in the Christian books that Mr Livingstone encouraged him to read.

David came up with a way to get some reading done while at work. He set up a book on part of the cotton spinning machine where it would not be in the way or cause a problem. Then as he passed back and forth doing his work as a piecer, he read sentence after sentence. Some days he was able to get quite a bit of reading done in that way.

Some of the other piecers who did not share David's interest in learning would pester him by throwing empty bobbins (spools that had held thread or yarn) to knock his book off the machine. They did not hesitate to suggest ways they thought he should use his time other than in reading and studying so much. Often, they started their suggestions with the words, 'I think ...':

'I think you should get your nose out of your books and have more fun,' one would advise.

'Yeah, Davey,' another would join in. 'I think you should hang around with us after work rather than running off to old McSkimming's school.'

'I think,' a third boy would add, 'you should forget about learning things like Latin and arithmetic. Those'll never do you any good anyway.'

When David grew tired of their suggestions he would sometimes respond with a playful grin: 'You *think*! I can *think* and *act* for myself; don't need anybody to think for me, I assure you.'

Though David's free time was very limited, he did not spend all his time working or studying. Nor did he always have his nose in a book. His scientific interests led him to go exploring for new types of plants or rocks. Through the years he and his two brothers often explored the surrounding countryside. They would gather different kinds of plants and herbs, then bring them home to identify them with the help of a couple of botany books.

On one of their outings, the Livingstone brothers went down into a limestone quarry. David was amazed and delighted as he discovered shell fossils in the rocks. 'How ever did these shells come into these rocks?' he asked a quarry worker.

The man shrugged his shoulders and offered a simple explanation: 'When God made the rocks, He made the shells in them.' David was not convinced that answer was correct.

Becoming a Christian and a Missionary

For a time when David was around twelve years of age, he became deeply concerned about his sinful spiritual condition. 'I wish I could have my heart and mind changed by receiving God's truth,' he thought to himself. 'I've been taught about God's offer of the gift of salvation. But I'm not good enough to receive such a great blessing from the Lord.'

He often shed tears in secret over his sinful condition. But he never told anyone what he was thinking and feeling about these matters. As a result, people were not able to help him with his spiritual struggles.

Over time David's concerns subsided. Through his teenage years he gave his time and attention to his work, his studies and his scientific interests. However, his heart was not fully at peace because of troubling thoughts he continued to have about his unspiritual condition.

When David was fourteen years old, he and John went to live with their grandparents in a cottage not far from the tenement building. That allowed the rest of the Livingstone family to have a little more space in their small one-room apartment.

After David turned eighteen, he was promoted to be a spinner at the cotton factory. He now operated the heavy machinery that spun cotton into thread or yarn. That job paid better but put much more strain on his body.

Throughout his boyhood David's parents had been careful to teach him about God's gift of salvation made possible through Jesus Christ's death on the cross. But it was not until he was nineteen years of age that he came to understand his own need to trust in Christ for forgiveness and salvation from sin. When David wrote many years later about his coming to saving faith in Christ, he was careful to add that God's mercy and grace allowed him to do so.

The Livingstones had always been part of the Church of Scotland congregation in Blantyre. But the same year that David became a Christian, the family started attending the independent Congregational Church in Hamilton, three miles from Blantyre.

Two years later, when David was twenty-one years old, he read a book written by an early missionary to China named Karl Gutzlaff. Mr Gutzlaff wrote about his journeys along the coast of China, where he preached the good news of salvation and passed out Christian literature to groups of people who were interested in what he had to share. He used medicine to help treat some of the physical problems that people had, which led them to be more willing to listen to his spiritual message.

Gutzlaff also urged more missionaries to come to China. China was then the largest country in the world with a population of 400 million people. There were almost no Christian missionaries or Chinese Christians in China in that day.

Thinking about all this, David decided: 'I will dedicate my life to go to China to minister to the spiritual and physical needs of people. Like Karl Gutzlaff, I'll combine missionary and medical ministry. I'll need to get a medical education, however.'

It took David two more years to save up enough money to pay for his first year of college. At last, in the autumn of 1836, at age twenty-three, he began his studies at Anderson College in Glasgow.

At the beginning of his second year of studies in Glasgow, some of his friends encouraged him: 'You should look into serving with the London Missionary Society (LMS). Its main goal is to spread the message of salvation to various parts of the world. It accepts missionaries from different kinds of churches. The LMS would provide you with training to be a missionary and would give you guidance in deciding where you will serve.'

Livingstone contacted the Directors of the LMS, and eventually they accepted him as one of their missionary trainees. Late in the summer of 1838, when

David was twenty-five years old, he moved to Chipping Ongar, a town about thirty miles northeast of London, England. There he and six other missionary students studied under a minister named Richard Cecil. They studied theology (what the Bible teaches on different spiritual subjects) as well as Hebrew and Greek, the languages in which the Old and New Testaments were first written. The students also had opportunities to preach in village churches near Chipping Ongar.

In January 1840, David moved to London to complete his medical training. He learned how to treat ailments and diseases with medicine or surgery. He was also trained as a doctor to assist women in giving birth to their babies.

Livingstone still wanted to serve as a missionary in China, but the London Missionary Society had not yet started a work there. 'We think you should serve instead in southern Africa,' the LMS Directors informed David. 'We already have a strong work established there and need more missionaries.' In addition, at that time Britain and China were fighting against each other in what was called the Opium War. China was closed to British missionaries for the time being.

A well-known missionary couple named Robert and Mary Moffat was back in England at that time. They had served for more than twenty years in southern Africa with the LMS and planned to return there. Mr Moffat was holding many missionary meetings in England, and large crowds of people came to hear him speak.

One day Moffat visited the boardinghouse where David and several other missionary trainees were living in London. David was more than interested in Moffat's missionary work and asked him questions about it whenever he came to visit. 'Where will you be speaking next?' David would also ask Mr Moffat. Then he would go and listen to him speak at those public preaching meetings.

'Do you think I would make a good missionary for Africa?' Livingstone asked Moffat on one occasion.

'I believe you would be,' Moffat responded. 'But I would encourage you not to go to an old missionary station where other missionaries are already serving. Instead, go to a new location where no other missionary has ever served.'

'Where would you advise me to go?' David questioned further.

'Well,' replied Moffat, 'I serve at Kuruman, which is the LMS's northernmost mission station in Africa. It is more than 500 miles from the southern coast of Africa. But there is a vast plain still further north beyond Kuruman. I have sometimes seen there, in the morning sun, the smoke of a thousand villages, where no missionary has ever yet been.'

'What is the use of my waiting for the end of this abominable Opium War in China?' David responded. 'I will go at once to Africa.'

That November Livingstone was licensed as a Medical Doctor. A few days later, in a church service held in London, he was publicly commissioned to serve as an ordained missionary in Africa with the London Missionary Society.

David and another missionary couple, Rev and Mrs William Ross, departed from London aboard a sailing ship named the *George* on December 8, 1840. They arrived at Simon's Bay near Cape Town, South Africa, on March 14, 1841, five days before David's twenty-eighth birthday.

The *George* then carried them 450 miles further east along the southern coast of Africa to the town of Port Elizabeth at Algoa Bay. There Livingstone and the Rosses had two large wagons built, which would transport them to Kuruman. They bought twenty-four oxen, as a dozen oxen were needed to pull each big wagon. They hired a few Africans to assist them in driving the wagons and managing the oxen. In addition, they bought food and other supplies which they would need for the long journey and after reaching Kuruman.

They set out from Port Elizabeth on May 20. Since they could not travel in a straight line, the journey to Kuruman was around 600 miles and lasted ten weeks. The ox-drawn wagons lumbered along at a top speed of just two miles per hour. By comparison, a person walking at a steady pace can usually walk three or four miles in an hour. At last they reached Kuruman on the final day of July, nearly eight months after they had sailed from England.

First Ministry Journeys
in Africa

Kuruman was located in a broad valley on a vast, high plain located 4,350 feet above sea level. A powerful spring three miles from Kuruman provided the town with a continuous supply of fresh water. Many years earlier Robert Moffat and his missionary partners had founded Kuruman, building sturdy stone houses and a stone church there. They also planted gardens, vineyards and fruit trees. Around 900 people now lived in that area, most of whom were Africans who belonged to various Bechuana tribes.

The Bechuana had many towns and villages in that part of Africa. Some of the Bechuana tribes were open to the possibility of missionaries coming to live with them, while others were not. Those unreceptive tribes knew that the missionaries did not approve of polygamy (when a man has more than one wife at the same time). Many of the Bechuana men kept several wives. However, some of the other tribes thought that if missionaries and other white men came, they would bring trading goods that the Africans desired to have. Plus, they hoped the white men would sell them guns which they could use to protect themselves from their enemies.

During the second half of October and all of November 1841, Livingstone and another missionary named Rogers Edwards made a circular journey of 700 miles in the territory above Kuruman. They were accompanied by two African Christian teachers from Kuruman. Though they never got more than 250 miles directly north of Kuruman, it was further in that direction than any other missionaries had ever been.

They traveled through hundreds of miles of dreary wilderness where the only plants they saw were thorn bushes and camel thorn trees. Now and then they spotted herds of wild horses, giraffes, ostriches and different kinds of antelope. They also saw a number of lions, which sometimes came close to their wagons, especially at night. However, the lions never bothered them, except to startle them out of their sleep with a powerful roar.

The nicest spot the two missionaries visited on that journey was the location where the Bakhatla (one of the many Bechuana tribes) were then living. The Bakhatla resided in a large valley between two mountain ranges, about 220 miles northeast of Kuruman. The valley had several freshwater springs and lots of pastureland for the Bakhatla's cattle. Many trees grew in the valley and large numbers of rhinoceros, water buffalo and zebra grazed there.

Near the end of that journey, Livingstone and his companions stopped at a large village about 150 miles from Kuruman. David doctored the sore eyes of the local chief who was most thankful for the treatment he received. After the missionaries left that village, they had gone about ten miles when a young girl of eleven or twelve years of age caught up with them and sat down under David's wagon.

'I am an orphan,' she explained. 'After my parents died, my older sister took care of me. But when she too died, another family took possession of me. They plan to sell me as soon as I am old enough to become a wife.'

'What will you do?' the missionaries asked her.

'I must run away and go live with some friends near Kuruman.'

'But it is many miles to Kuruman.'

'That does not matter,' she stated with determination. Looking directly at Livingstone, she added, 'I plan to walk the entire way behind the white man's wagon if he will allow me to do so.'

David gave her some food to eat. However, a short while later he heard her sobbing, as if her heart would break. A man with a gun had just arrived, having come to take her back to the village.

David was not sure what to do. Just then, one of the African Christians from Kuruman, whose name was Pomore, jumped up to help the girl. Pomore was the son of a chief and was used to handling situations with a degree of authority. He soon convinced the man from the village to leave the girl with them.

She had been given many strings of beads, which the Africans highly valued, to help her look more attractive. In that way she would bring a higher bridal price for the family that was selling her. But she now took off all the beads and handed them back to the man who had come from the village. 'Here are all your beads,' she told him, then added, 'Now please, go away and leave me alone.'

The man was not at all happy, but he did so. Livingstone and his companions took the girl with them. They delivered her to her acquaintances near Kuruman who would take good care of her.

While on their recent journey and after returning to Kuruman, people came from great distances to receive medical treatment from Livingstone. Some people walked 130 miles to be helped by him. Sometimes his wagon was surrounded with people requiring his help. 'Doing this helps me learn the Sechuana language more rapidly,' David told his friends, 'because I am always speaking to the people in their native tongue.' Sechuana was the language spoken by the Bechuana.

The most common complaints David treated were people's indigestion, eye infections from blowing sand, and rheumatism (pain in the joints and muscles). He also assisted women in giving birth to their babies when the mothers were in difficulty. He removed a number of tumors (abnormal growths) from under people's skin. He once removed a very large tumor the size of a child's head from the base of a man's neck!

In February of the following year, 1842, Livingstone set out again from Kuruman to revisit some of the Bechuana tribes to the north. The same two African teachers from Kuruman went with him as well as two other Africans to drive the wagon. David and the teachers shared the message of salvation with each of the tribes they visited.

They stayed for a month at the village of a chief named Bubi. Chief Bubi's village was located atop a high, steep hill overlooking a tree-covered plain. A short distance away, a large stream wound around the bottom of the hill.

'Allow me to show you,' Livingstone said to Bubi and his people, 'how you can have a constant supply of water for your village and your gardens. You will no longer need to rely on witchdoctors to bring rain.' David further stated to Bubi: 'Provide me with men to do the work. I will teach them how to dam up part of the stream and dig an irrigation canal to bring water to your gardens at the base of the hill on which your village sits.'

The missionary had not planned to carry out such a project during his visit to the tribes, so he did not have any of the tools he thought they needed. They instead used sharpened sticks to dig the canal and carried away the dirt in animal skins, turtle shells and wooden bowls. They built a large dam made of stones and earth. The canal ended up being over 400 feet long, one yard wide and, in places, four feet deep. When they came to large boulders, they had to dig around them, so the watercourse ended up looking like a slithering snake.

Bubi's men worked hard and willingly. Even the chief's own witchdoctor worked at the project laughing loudly as he said, 'How clever the foreigner is that he can make rain in this way!' The other workmen, who were all impressed with the project, exclaimed, 'A great, great, great work is this of the foreigner.'

Livingstone visited several other Bechuana tribes on this journey. When he arrived back in Kuruman in mid-June, he had traveled over 1,000 miles and had been away for four months and one week. In all that time he had not been around any Europeans and had constantly spoken Sechuana with the Africans. He now found that he could speak their language quite freely.

Due to fighting that broke out among the Bechuana tribes to the north of Kuruman, David was not able to leave on his third journey to visit them till February of the following year, 1843. While teaching a chief named Sechele and his people, Livingstone began to describe the scene spoken of in Revelation 20:11-15. Those Bible verses speak of God sitting on His great white throne, earth and sky fleeing away, and every person standing before God to be judged.

Sechele responded to this teaching by saying, 'You startle me. These words make all my bones to shake. I have no more strength in me.'

Then the chief asked a hard question: 'But my forefathers were living at the same time yours were. So how is it that they did not send them word about these terrible things sooner? They all passed away into darkness without knowing where they were going.'

'There are many large groups of people in my own country,' David answered, 'who, like you, love their sins greatly. My ancestors spent many years trying to convince them to turn away from their sins to God. Many people refused to do so and were lost.'

The missionary continued: 'But we now wish to tell all the world about the Savior Jesus. We Christians first came to the south coast of Africa by boats, and have slowly spread the knowledge of God from there northward. I believe that, as Christ Jesus Himself has said, the spiritual light of God's good news of salvation will yet come to the whole world.'

Sechele pointed north and west in the direction of the Kalahari Desert, which stretched out for hundreds of miles beyond where he and his tribe lived. 'You never can cross that country to the tribes beyond,' he stated. 'It is utterly impossible even for us black men, except in certain seasons, when more than the usual supply of rain falls, and a very large growth of watermelons follows. Even we who know the country would certainly perish there without them.'

Africa's Greatest Explorer

'I still believe that what Christ has said is true,' David replied. 'Even though those tribes are hard to reach, the message of God's salvation will someday come to them as well.'

Attacked by a Lion

David arrived back at Kuruman in June 1843. Two months later he and Rogers Edwards returned to the Bakhatla region, which the missionaries had visited in November 1841. There the Bakhatla tribe lived in a large, well-watered valley between two mountain ranges.

Livingstone and Edwards met with Moseeealele (pronounced Mo-see-a-le-le), the Bakhatla chief, and around 100 of his men. 'We desire you to come and live among us,' the Bakhatla told the missionaries. 'We will sell you a large piece of property with plenty of woods, pastureland and water, where you can build your houses and plant your gardens.' The location for the new mission station was called Mabotsa.

The missionaries then traveled back to Kuruman. Robert and Mary Moffat, along with some of their children, were returning there after their recent years in England. Livingstone rode more than 150 miles south on horseback to meet the Moffats and to help them in any way he could as they completed their journey to Kuruman.

In January of the following year, 1844, Livingstone and Mr and Mrs Edwards returned to Mabotsa. They were accompanied by Mebalwe, a faithful deacon from the Kuruman church, who had come to assist them in their building and teaching ministries at Mabotsa. Immediately after arriving there, the missionaries hired seven Bakhatla to assist them in digging an irrigation canal to supply their gardens with water.

Mabotsa was, at that point, being terrorized by aggressive lions which leaped into the Bakhatla's cattle pens at night and destroyed their cows. They even attacked the herds in broad daylight, which lions normally did not do. It was well known that if one member of a lion pride were killed, the others would usually leave the area.

During the daytime on Wednesday, February 7, a lion killed nine sheep and goats on a hill directly across from the mission house. The men of the village immediately rushed over to try and form a circle around the lion in order to kill it with their spears. Livingstone and Mebalwe went with the village men to try and shoot the lion with their rifles, but they were not able to take a shot without endangering the men.

As David and Mebalwe began to make their way back to their home, they spotted another lion, about thirty yards away, sitting on a rock and partly hidden by a small bush. David took careful aim at the animal's body through the bush then fired both barrels of his rifle.

'He is shot! He is shot!' some of the men shouted. 'Let us go to him!' others yelled.

Livingstone could see the lion's tail standing straight up in fury behind the bush. 'Stop a little,' he told the men, 'till I reload my gun.'

But as he was reloading, he heard a shout and looked up just in time to see the lion leaping upon him. It bit down on his left upper arm, just below the shoulder, crushing the humerus bone. David had been standing on a slight rise, and both he and the lion crashed to the ground below.

The lion growled close to his ear and shook him like a terrier dog shakes a rat. All this left Livingstone in a state of shock. He felt like he was in a dream in which he felt no pain or fear. However, he was still aware of all that was happening.

Livingstone turned his head to relieve the heavy weight from one of the lion's large paws pressing down on the back of his head. Mebalwe was standing only ten or fifteen yards away, trying to shoot the lion without harming David. Although when Mebalwe's gun failed to fire, the lion attacked the African and bit his thigh. Another brave African tried to spear the lion as it was biting Mebalwe. The beast turned on that third man and bit him on the shoulder. Then suddenly the lion fell down dead from the two gunshot wounds it had received from David's rifle.

'This is the largest lion we have ever seen!' the Bakhatla exclaimed.

Men came running to help care for Livingstone and the two Africans who had been bitten. Mr Edwards came to help David, but since Edwards was not a doctor, he did not know how to reset the splintered bone in Livingstone's upper arm. David, who was now in great pain, needed to tell Edwards how to reset the bone the best he could.

The lion's bite left eleven ugly wounds in the skin of Livingstone's arm. Those wounds were carefully washed, then David was laid in a small African hut to rest and recover. After several days he was well enough to get up and walk around. But it took many more weeks for his arm to heal.

In July, five months after being attacked by the lion, Livingstone traveled back to Kuruman. His main reason for doing so appears to have been to ask Robert Moffat's oldest daughter to marry him. Miss Moffat, who was then twenty-three years old, was named Mary after her mother. She had returned from England to Africa with her parents the previous year. David had gotten to know her while traveling with the Moffats to Kuruman at the end of that year.

Mary had been born and raised in Africa. Being the oldest of the Moffats' ten children, she was used to helping her mother care for the younger children and their home. As part of her education Mary had been trained as a teacher. After returning to Kuruman, she was placed in charge of the school for early elementary students. She spoke the Sechuana language 'like a native', and the African children were fond of her.

David had thought much about Mary during his time away from her in Mabotsa. He was impressed and attracted by her many good qualities. He also came to have romantic feelings for her in his heart. He concluded that she would make an excellent wife, mother and missionary partner.

David revealed his thoughts and feelings about Mary to her while visiting in Kuruman that July. One day while they were out for a walk, they paused under an almond tree. 'Mary,' he said quietly, 'you have become very dear to me. I have little of this world's goods to offer you. But I do pledge to love and care for you. I believe we can be happy serving the Lord together. Would you agree to be my wife and share my life?'

'Yes, with all my heart,' Mary responded warmly, smiling up at him. 'I would be honored.'

They decided to marry early the following year, after David had built a home for them to live in at Mabotsa. Upon returning there, he set to work building a good-sized house for Mary and himself. At first he planned to build the walls of the house entirely of stone. But when the thick stone walls were about chest high, he suffered an accident that led him to change his plan. One day a heavy stone fell from the top of the wall. Without thinking about it, David reached out to catch it with his left hand, thus refracturing the bone in the upper portion of that arm. It was the same arm that had been bitten by the lion.

Livingstone's left arm never fully recovered from that second injury. Although he could use the arm to pound nails with a hammer or to lift heavy weights, for the remainder of his life his left humerus bone never healed solid. Instead, the bone had a hinge effect in it. When he stretched out his arm with his palm up and placed weight on it, part of his humerus bone raised up like it was going to poke through the skin. As a result, he was no longer able to shoot a rifle while supporting the weight of its barrel with his left hand and arm. Rather, he needed to learn to shoot while bearing the weight of the gun with his right hand and arm.

Work on the house resumed while David's arm recovered from its second injury. He and the Africans assisting him now used layers of sunbaked mud rather than stones in continuing to raise the walls to their full height. After drying in the sun, the mud walls were nearly as hard as brick.

David and Mary were married in Kuruman on January 2, 1845. He was thirty-one years old and she was twenty-three. They arrived at their new home in Mabotsa the final week of March.

Leading a Chief to Faith
in Christ

Though Livingstone intended to minister in Mabotsa for a time, he thought the new mission station reached too few Africans to justify needing two missionaries plus their African Christian helpers. He had already informed Robert Moffat and some of his other fellow missionaries of his desire to eventually start another mission work among the Bakwains, a different Bechuana tribe located north of Mabotsa.

In August David and Mary decided they would relocate to Chonuane, the village of the most prominent Bakwain chief, Sechele. Chonuane was about forty miles north and a little east of Mabotsa. Livingstone had ministered briefly to Sechele and his people at Chonuane a little over two years earlier. Now, during the closing months of 1845, David spent much of his time in Chonuane, building a house and starting a school.

The school met first thing each morning in the town's public meeting place. Sechele himself faithfully attended. He studied hard and learned quickly. He learned the entire alphabet, both capital and lowercase letters, in just two days, and was soon reading and spelling two-syllable words.

Meanwhile, Mary was still living in Mabotsa, where she continued to teach the young children, as she had ever since arriving there. As Mr Edwards was away for several months to purchase needed supplies at the coast, David led Sunday worship services whenever he was back at Mabotsa.

David and Mary's first child was born in January of 1846. He was named Robert Moffat after his grandfather. Following Bechuana custom, David and Mary now would be called not by their own first names, but by the name of their firstborn child, with a prefix indicating father or mother. Thus, David was commonly called Ra-Robert, meaning 'Father of Robert', while Mary was named Ma-Robert, 'Mother of Robert'.

A couple months after Robert's birth, the Livingstones moved to Chonuane. Mebalwe and another African Christian teacher from Kuruman named Paul moved there also, to assist them with their ministries.

Like the other Bechuana chiefs and tribes, Chief Sechele and the Bakwains believed strongly in rainmaking. When tribes needed rain for their crops, their chief or a hired rainmaker would burn medicine made of roots and plant bulbs. 'The smoke from the medicine,' the Africans explained, 'rises and enters the clouds, healing them and causing them to rain.'

'But your rain medicines produce no effect that can be seen,' Livingstone pointed out. 'The smoke of your medicines rises up to the clouds, but the rain still does not come. Look how very long it has been since you have received any rain.'

'Your medicines,' the tribesmen responded, 'also produce no immediate effect when you give them. But they enter into a person's inward parts, do their work, and then the cure follows many days later. In the same way, our rain medicines enter into the clouds, heal them, and we have rain later.'

Sechele was his tribe's chief rainmaker and had great confidence in his own powers to bring rain. However, that year, 1846, brought a terrible drought to that part of Africa. The clouds passed all around Chonuane but never brought rain to it. When 1847 began with no sign of rain anywhere, David asked Sechele, 'Do you intend to make rain this year?'

'You will never see me doing that kind of work again,' the chief replied.

A highly respected rainmaker was called from a great distance. 'Give me a sheep in exchange for my services,' he stated, 'and I promise to bring you rain in the next two weeks.' After the two weeks passed but no rain came, he said: 'Give me another sheep and I promise to bring you rain. I just need a little more time.'

Some of the people laughed at him and asked: 'Why should we give you another sheep when you were not able to bring rain the first time? Why should we believe that you will be able to keep your promise this time?'

But other townspeople, who feared the rainmaker, said: 'Do not laugh at the rainmaker or make him angry. Do you want him to drive away the rain rather than bring it to us? Don't you know that he can also bring lightning to kill people?'

In time Sechele and his wives became the best students Livingstone and the African Christian teachers had. The chief was able to read the Sechuana New Testament quite well and was always interested in learning more about what he had read.

David and Mary's second child, a daughter whom they named Agnes (after David's mother), was born the middle of that June. One month later, due to the continued lack of rain and food at Chonuane, Sechele's tribe accepted Livingstone's advice to move their village to Kolobeng, around forty miles further north. There 'a fine stream' flowed from the nearby hills and would provide them with plenty of water.

'I will have my own people construct the town's school building,' Sechele announced. 'It will also be used as a meeting place for church services. I desire to build a house for God, the defender of my town.' More than 200 of the chief's men soon completed the meetinghouse.

Livingstone, Mebalwe and Paul continued to hold school for adults and older youth early in the morning. Throughout the day they worked on different building projects that needed to be done, including constructing their own homes. Each evening they led a prayer meeting and read a Bible passage at Sechele's home. Any villagers who wanted to do so were invited to join the chief and his family for those evening meetings. Mary started an early elementary school and a sewing school for the village children.

Sechele saw that Livingstone strongly desired his people to believe and accept the teachings of Jesus which the missionary faithfully shared with them. 'Do you imagine these people will ever believe by your merely talking to them?' Sechele once asked David. 'I can make them do nothing except by thrashing them.' The chief then made a surprising suggestion: 'And if you like, I shall call my headmen [tribal leaders], and with our rhinoceros-hide whips we will soon make them all believe together!'

For many months Sechele had shown great interest in Christian teaching, but he would not commit to becoming a Christian as he could not bring himself to turn away from polygamy. To do that he would have to go back to living with only his first wife.

In July of 1848, however, he suddenly professed his faith in Christ as his Savior from sin. 'And I wish to be baptized to show my people that I am an obedient follower of Jesus. I will now remain married only to my first wife.' His other former wives were sent back to their families to be cared for by them. They returned to their families with all their possessions, as well as with new clothes which Sechele provided for them to show that he was not upset with them.

Sechele's tribe opposed his decisions to become a Christian and to no longer practice polygamy. Tribal meetings were held at night to try to frighten the chief and force him to change his mind. His own people cursed him bitterly. When he was baptized on the first day of October, many of his people shed tears of sorrow.

Despite all that opposition, Sechele stayed strong in his faith in the Lord Jesus. In the years that followed he was a faithful Christian witness to the people of his tribe and tried to lead them to believe in Jesus as their Savior.

Challenging Journeys Far Further North

During the years Livingstone had been ministering to Sechele and the Bakwains at Chonuane and Kolobeng, the missionary also made three journeys to other African tribes. They lived more than 250 miles to the east, in an area called the Transvaal. A group of Dutch farmers called Boers lived in that region north of the Vaal River and ruled over the tribes there. The Boers made the Africans work for them without pay and took many of their cattle and sheep without paying for them. They also attacked and killed some of the Africans who did not cooperate with them or made them their slaves.

The Boers did not want David to influence the Transvaal tribes by bringing the Bible's teachings to them. They also wanted to expand their rule so they could control the tribes around Kolobeng and north of there. 'Livingstone must leave the Kolobeng region,' they demanded. They also commanded Chief Sechele, 'You must not allow any white men to travel past you, further north into Africa.'

David and Mary's third child, a son whom they named Thomas, was born at Kolobeng in March of

1849. Five or six weeks later Mary and the children, accompanied by Mebalwe and his family, went to Kuruman to visit her parents. They stayed at Kuruman for several weeks while David took a journey far further north in Africa than he had ever been before.

Despite the threats of the Boers, Livingstone planned to travel through the Kalahari Desert and to a large lake far to the northwest of Kolobeng. No white person had ever crossed the Kalahari to that lake, which was named Lake Ngami. No one knew how many hundreds of miles the lake was from Kolobeng. David longed to go there to take the good news of salvation to the tribes that lived at the lake and beyond it.

Livingstone was joined on this journey by William Oswell and Mungo Murray, whom he had first met at Mabotsa four years earlier when they were on a hunting expedition. Oswell was from England and Murray from Scotland. They were experienced travelers and hunters in Africa.

Livingstone, Oswell and Murray took with them nearly twenty African men to help them on the journey. They also had some eighty oxen to take turns pulling the wagons loaded with supplies, as well as twenty horses and a number of dogs. As they made their way through the eastern side of the Kalahari Desert, they were in danger of running out of water for all those people and animals.

At one location named Serotli they found a few dry hollowed-out spots in the ground where it looked like buffaloes and rhinoceroses had earlier rolled in the mud. In the corner of one of those spots was a little water, which would have been quickly lapped up by the dogs if they had not been driven away from it. Their head guide, who had grown up in the desert, declared confidently, 'There is plenty of water here.'

Other guides began to eagerly scrape sand out of the hollow with their hands. David and a few others helped dig out the sand using shovels. The guides earnestly warned them, 'When we get down to the hard layer of sand at the bottom, be careful not to break through it, or the water will go away.' They dug out two pits, both about six feet deep and six feet wide.

When they reached the hard layer of sand, they discovered water flowing in on all sides, close to the line where the soft and hard sand met. They allowed the pits to fill up with water, and by that evening had enough for the men and horses. The eighty oxen were taken back to a watering spot they had passed earlier. By the time the oxen returned to Serotli a few days later, there was enough water for them as well.

By early July they thought they were nearing Lake Ngami. However, they had really traveled only half the 600-mile distance between Kolobeng and Lake Ngami. On July 4 they were greatly encouraged to come to a large river. 'This is the Zouga River,' the local tribesmen informed them. 'You can follow it all the way to Lake Ngami.'

As they neared Lake Ngami, a sizeable stream flowed into the Zouga from the north. It was named the Tamunakle. It was so cold and clean that Livingstone and his companions thought its waters must have started from melting snow in a mountainous region.

'Where does this stream come from?' David asked the Africans.

They answered: 'Oh, from a country full of rivers – so many no one can tell their number. It is a land full of large trees also.'

That response confirmed statements the Bakwains had earlier made to Livingstone that the vast region beyond the Kalahari Desert and Lake Ngami was full of many large rivers and sizeable tribes. Before this, people in Europe and America wrongly thought that the entire inland region of southern Africa was an enormous desert with no water or people, like the gigantic Sahara Desert in northern Africa.

On this journey Livingstone, Oswell and Murray became the first white men to have crossed the Kalahari Desert and to discover Lake Ngami, which they finally reached on August 1. David was pleased with their accomplishments and discoveries. But he was far more enthused about the tremendous spiritual benefits that could potentially be brought to southern Africa's immense inland region as a result of their discoveries. 'The many rivers of this area could be used as highways to bring the message of salvation to the numerous large tribes that live here,' he thought.

In mid-April of the following year, 1850, Livingstone set out on a second journey to Lake Ngami. This time he took Mary and their children with him. 'Last year I was unable to visit the powerful Makololo tribe that lives 200 miles north of Lake Ngami,' he told Mary. 'So I would like to visit them this year.' However, developments at the lake again prevented him from doing so.

A few days before reaching Lake Ngami, the Livingstones received news that a group of Englishmen who had recently gone there in search of ivory had all fallen seriously ill with fever. Hurrying on to the lake, they were saddened to learn that a young artist who was traveling with the group to make sketches of the lake and surrounding country had already died. David treated the other members of the party with medicine, and they all recovered.

David and Mary took their young children to see the broad south side of the lake. The children played gleefully in the water. The next day, though, their daughter Agnes and son Thomas, as well as Mebalwe and some of their hired servants, came down with fever. They became very ill. Thankfully, God protected their lives and allowed all of them to recover.

During the opening week of August, just seven days after the Livingstones arrived back at Kolobeng, Mary gave birth to their second daughter, whom they named Elizabeth. Two weeks after the baby's birth, the right side of Mary's face developed a paralysis. She could not wink her right eye or smile with that side of her lips. Mercifully, over time the paralysis gradually went away.

Not long after Baby Elizabeth's birth, an epidemic spread through Kolobeng that affected many people's lungs and made it hard for them to breathe. Baby Elizabeth came down with the illness when one month old, then died two weeks later. With great sadness the Livingstones buried her tiny body in a grove of mimosa trees. They believed that her soul had gone to live with God in Heaven, and that there they would see her again someday. They were comforted by that assurance.

In the final week of April 1851, David again set out with his family in yet another attempt to reach the Makololo tribe north of Lake Ngami. William Oswell had returned to help the Livingstones on this journey.

After their traveling party left a final rainwater pool on June 9, the journey became extremely difficult. They had to constantly use their axes to cut a path through an area of thick bush that stretched out for many miles. Sixteen oxen were harnessed together to pull the heavy wagons through the sandy soil. The path through the bush was sometimes so winding that the Livingstones could not see the lead oxen in the span that was pulling their wagon.

Then they came to a broad plain of low, thorny scrub bushes that stretched out as far as the eye could see. No animal, bird or insect could be seen, and everything was totally quiet. Their guide, who had lost his way, started following old, deserted elephant trails in all directions. He then disappeared altogether. They unyoked the oxen which immediately rushed off in search of water. Livingstone and Oswell remained at the wagons with Mary and the children, while their African attendants all went looking for water and the oxen.

The supply of water in the wagons had been wasted by one of the hired servants, and by the afternoon only a small amount remained, just enough for the children. 'This was a bitterly anxious night,' David later revealed. 'The idea of the children perishing before our eyes was terrible.'

The next morning, the less there was of water, the thirstier the children became. It seemed to David that it would almost have been a relief to him if Mary had accused him of being totally to blame for this catastrophe. Yet, she spoke not a single word of reproach against him. The tears in her eyes showed the agony in her soft mother's heart for her children.

That morning David and Oswell went looking for their servants and found them returning with a supply of water which the oxen had led them to, at a river several miles away. Unfortunately, along the way some of the oxen had been bitten by tsetse flies. Tsetse were about the same size as common houseflies, but their bite was deadly to different types of livestock. Nobody knew in those days that the bite of the tsetse fly could also cause sleeping sickness in humans.

Within days, the oxen began showing signs of having been bitten by the insects, and a few weeks later they started dying off. Though David and his companions did all they could to avoid the tsetse and to keep the flies off the cattle, forty-three 'fine oxen' died from their bites during that journey.

On June 19 their party reached a Makololo village on the northern side of the Chobe River. That river was a major tributary of the mighty Zambesi River, which it joined to the northeast. Two days later Livingstone and Oswell were taken in a canoe twenty-five or more miles downriver to meet Sebituane, the Makololo chief. Sebituane's primary residence was at the town of Linyanti, but Livingstone and Oswell met him at the island village of one of the chief's thirty wives.

For almost three decades Sebituane and the Makololo had been involved in constant warfare, either attacking or being attacked by other tribes. The Makololo assaulted other tribes, stole their livestock and forced them to live under their authority. Sebituane and the Makololo had come to rule over a large area that stretched out for hundreds of miles around the Chobe River and the upper region of the Zambesi River.

That Sunday, June 22, Livingstone held two Bible teaching services with the chief and his people. Just a day or two later Sebituane fell seriously ill with pneumonia, which he had battled before. David visited Sebituane daily and could clearly see the chief's condition was becoming grave. Livingstone offered to help treat Sebituane but the chief's physicians declined to accept his assistance.

When Livingstone visited Sebituane on Sunday, July 6, the dying chief said, 'Come near and see if I am any longer a man. I am done.'

'Your disease is very dangerous,' David stated. 'But through God's Son, Jesus Christ, we can come to have the hope of life even after death.'

'Why do you speak of death?' one of Sebituane's doctors immediately interrupted, then declared, 'Sebituane will never die.'

The Makololo always avoided referring to the death of their chief. Livingstone knew that if he continued to speak about it, the Makololo would think he wished to hasten Sebituane's death by discussing it. After sitting with Sebituane a while longer, David silently prayed, asking God to be merciful to the dying chief, then got up and left. Sebituane died the next morning.

Livingstone and Oswell traveled 130 miles north of Linyanti on horseback and arrived at the Zambesi River on August 4. They were the first white men to discover that upper portion of the Zambesi, which from that point flowed another 1,000 miles to the Indian Ocean on the southeast coast of Africa. At this northerly location discovered by Livingstone and Oswell, the Zambesi was 400 yards wide and quite deep. As the two men gazed out over the river, they kept exclaiming, 'How glorious!', 'How magnificent!', 'How beautiful!' David later added, 'And grand beyond description it really was.'

While traveling among the Makololo, Livingstone saw that many of them wore clothes made of woolen and cotton cloth. They had gotten the cloth by trading with the Mambari, an African tribe that resided in the territory of Angola in western Africa.

The Mambari were slave traders and had spent several months with Sebituane and the Makololo the previous year, 1850.

When the Makololo offered to trade cattle and ivory for rifles and cloth, the Mambari refused, saying they wanted only boy slaves around fourteen years of age. The Makololo then attacked one of the neighboring tribes in the region, keeping that tribe's cattle for themselves and capturing some 200 youths whom they traded to the Mambari as slaves.

Livingstone and Oswell protested to the Makololo against slave trading, and the tribesmen seemed to understand that it was wrong. Appealing to the Makololos' strong sense of affection for their own families, David tried to persuade them by pointing out: 'It is not right to break up families by taking children from their parents or parents from their children and selling them as slaves. If anyone did that to you and your children, you would feel totally wronged and would strongly oppose it.' The Makololo readily agreed, stating, 'What you say is good and correct.'

At the end of that journey, as the Livingstones and Oswell made their way down the Zouga River back toward their home in Kolobeng, Mary gave birth to their third son. They named him William Oswell, after their friend and fellow traveler who had been so helpful to them.

Traveling among Friends and Foes

Livingstone desired to establish a missionary work among the Makololo. But he thought he would need two years, while living with the Makololo, to make the necessary preparations for a sustainable ministry to them.

'There is much fever in the Makololo territory,' David pointed out to Oswell, 'which is dangerous and deadly, even to some of the tribes who live in that region.'

'The fever would be far more deadly to white people coming into the area,' Oswell observed.

'Yes,' David agreed. 'That's why I need to find a healthy location there, where I and other missionaries can more safely settle with our families to minister.' Switching to another challenge, David added: 'So much time and money would be required to bring missionaries and all their necessary supplies the 1,500 or more miles from the southern coast to Makolololand.'

'The tsetse fly would make it nearly impossible for them to be brought by ox-drawn wagon,' Oswell noted realistically.

'I'll spend part of my time with the Makololo exploring the rivers of that region,' Livingstone stated. 'I need to determine if a waterway exists from either the west or east coast, by which people and goods could be brought to the interior more quickly, easily and affordably than can be done by the southerly overland route.'

David and Mary made the difficult decision that she would go to Britain with their young children during the two years he planned to be with the Makololo. In that way the children would be kept safe from dangerous African fevers and could receive their education in Britain. Many missionary families in the 1800s sent their children back to their home countries for the sake of the children's health and education.

The Livingstones traveled to Cape Town during the opening months of 1852. After Mary and the children sailed for England, David set out to return to the Makololo. A few days after he reached Kuruman near the end of August, deeply concerning news was received: 600 Boers on horseback, accompanied by 700 Africans whom they enlisted to help them, had attacked Sechele and the Bakwains at Limaoe. Sechele and his people had moved eight miles from Kolobeng to Limaoe a year earlier.

Around sixty Bakwains, including some women and children, were killed in the assault. As many as 200 women and perhaps even a greater number of children were taken as slaves. Around thirty Boers and their African associates were killed in the battle. At least two other tribes in the region, including the Bakhatla at Mabotsa, were also attacked by the Boers. Their villages were burned and their livestock was carried off.

A group of Boers also went to Kolobeng and ransacked the Livingstones' home there. They brought four wagons and hauled away the missionaries' furniture, dishware, tools and cattle. They tore the pages out of David's books and scattered them in front of the house. They also smashed all the medicine bottles and the windows of the house. In all, the Livingstones' possessions destroyed or stolen in the attack were worth nearly £300. That was equivalent to three years of David's salary as a missionary.

Not surprisingly, Livingstone had a hard time finding Africans who were willing to assist him in traveling through the territory where the Boers had recently attacked . However, in mid-December he was finally able to hire a few servants and to set out from Kuruman with his ox-drawn wagon.

They reached Linyanti, the Makololo's primary town, on May 23, 1853. The town's entire population of 6,000 or 7,000 people came out to welcome them. Sebituane's eighteen-year-old son, Sekeletu, had become the Makololos' new chief in place of his deceased father.

Despite experiencing his first-ever attack of malarial fever one week after arriving at Linyanti, David, Sekeletu and around 160 of the chief's men carried out a journey through the Barotse territory along part of the upper Zambesi River. This lasted for nine weeks during the months of July, August and September.

The Barotse were the group of tribes furthest to the west that were under the rule of Sekeletu and the Makololo. David suffered several more severe attacks of malaria in the Barotse country. He and his traveling companions also discovered that the deadly tsetse fly was present there. For both those reasons he concluded that a missionary work could not be established in that area.

After returning to Linyanti in mid-September, Livingstone began preparing for a journey to the west coast. He hoped to discover a route by which Christian missionaries and constructive trade (rather than destructive slave trading) could be brought to inland Africa. David and twenty-seven of Sekeletu's men set out for the coast on November 11. Sekeletu, who stayed behind in Linyanti, sent orders to the tribes over which he ruled: 'Provide the white man and my men with canoes for traveling up the Zambesi River. And supply them with oxen for food and to help carry their supplies.'

David had brought with him a device called a magic lantern, with which he could show large, lighted pictures on a screen of white cloth or canvas. (The magic lantern was like a simple video projector today, only its image was not that bright as it was illuminated by an oil lamp rather than by a high-powered electrical lightbulb.) David used the magic lantern to show pictures of key Bible events and to tell those important stories. The Africans were amazed at the white man's big, lighted pictures, and they traveled many miles to see them.

Some of the Makololo in the northwesterly part of Sekeletu's territory had recently attacked the villages of other tribes, killing and taking a number of people as slaves. Livingstone and his party were able to gather eighteen of those captives and return them to their own tribes. 'We return eighteen souls from captivity,' David reported, 'a thing never before performed in this part of Africa.'

After passing through the Makololo and Barotse regions, Livingstone's expedition entered the territory of the Balonda tribes. There they needed to leave the Zambesi River and continue their journey on foot, in a northwesterly direction through thick forests. In mid-January 1854, David's party arrived at the town of Shinte, the most powerful of all the Balonda chiefs.

A group of Portuguese and Mambari were also present at Shinte's town at that time. They had come to trade in the area for slaves, ivory and beeswax. Livingstone's men saw a group of young female slaves who had been chained together and were hoeing the ground in front of the Portuguese and Mambari camp to clear it of weeds and grass. This was the first time that most of David's men had seen slaves in chains. They were shocked and exclaimed about the slave traders,

'They are not men but beasts who treat their children in this way.'

One evening two children, ages seven and eight, went outside their parents' home, which was not far from Shinte's town, to gather firewood. They were kidnapped and sold to the slave traders camped nearby. Livingstone explained: 'This is a common practice wherever the slave traders go. Those who are unwilling to part with their own servants or children steal them from outlying hamlets and sell them by night. The slave traders only need to give a small amount of cloth in order to buy a slave.' The slave traders kept these newly purchased children out of sight and denied that they had them. When the children's parents protested, they received no help or compassion from either village leaders or slave traders.

One Sunday evening Livingstone showed the magic lantern pictures to Shinte and the leading men and women of his town. The first picture shown was of Abraham in Genesis 22 with his knife lifted over his son Isaac. Pointing to the large, illuminated image of Abraham on the screen, the Balonda men commented, 'He looks much more like a god than the idols of wood and clay which we worship.'

The women listened in silence, amazed at what they were seeing and hearing. But when David started to move the glass slide in the magic lantern to replace it with the next picture, the image of Abraham with his uplifted knife moved toward the people on that side of the screen. Fearing that the image might strike them with the knife, they all cried out for protection, 'Mother! Mother!' In their haste to escape, they tumbled over each other and over the little idol huts and tobacco bushes in Shinte's courtyard.

As Livingstone and his company continued their journey to the north and west, they came to a large region where one tribe after another demanded heavy payments in exchange for permission to pass through their territory. Up to that point most tribes had been willing to provide David's party with food in exchange for beads, which the Africans prized. Those tribes also allowed them to proceed through their districts without further payment.

Now, however, many tribes began to demand major items like an elephant tusk, an ox, a gun or even a man as a slave before granting permission to pass by. Livingstone's company needed to save their few oxen to feed themselves. They had only five guns, and those were needed for hunting and for protection. These men were willing to die for each other, if need be, rather than allow one of their number to be taken as a slave.

When their party arrived near the town of Chief Niambi, the foremost leader of the Chiboque tribes, they were nearly out of food so slaughtered one of their oxen. Following the custom of that region, they sent the hump with the ribs attached to Niambi as his portion of their meat. But the chief scorned the meat as being of little value and demanded instead a man, a tusk, a gun or some other expensive gift.

The next day Niambi and all his men came armed with their weapons to Livingstone's camp. David's men picked up their own weapons and stood on the defensive, while the young Chiboque men waved their short swords with 'great fury'.

Seeking to defuse the tense situation, the missionary sat down on his camp stool and laid his rifle across his knees. 'Come, friends,' he calmly and pleasantly said to Niambi and the chief's companions, as well as to his own Makololo men. 'Let's sit down together and discuss matters peacefully.' Eventually Niambi and some of his counselors sat down, as did some of David's men. However, the young Chiboque continued to stand while waving their swords and even pointing their guns at Livingstone and his associates.

'What guilt does my party have,' David asked Niambi, 'that led you and your men to come out armed against us?'

'One of your men,' Niambi asserted, indicating a Makololo leader in Livingstone's group named Pitsane, 'gave one of my people a piece of meat. But then while they were sitting by the fire, your man spit on the ground and a drop of it landed on my servant's foot.'

'Is this true?' David asked Pitsane.

'Yes,' Pitsane responded, 'but I only meant to spit on the ground. And only a drop hit the servant's foot.'

Turning back to Niambi, David said, 'I will pay a small fine for this accidental offense. But I must ask, do you really consider this a matter of guilt?'

'Yes, I do,' Niambi replied. 'And payment must be made to wipe away the offense.'

David got out one of his own white shirts and offered it to the chief as payment. Niambi seemed pleased with it, though his young men refused the offering and demanded a larger payment. The missionary added a bunch of beads, then a large handkerchief. Niambi seemed satisfied with each additional offering, but his counselors were not.

Every time a new demand was made, the chief's men rushed around brandishing their weapons. One young Chiboque warrior charged at David from behind and stopped his sword just over the missionary's head. David quickly turned and lifted the barrel of his rifle to the man's mouth, causing him to retreat.

Finally the Chiboque tribesmen demanded an ox. Livingstone's companions urged him to give one in order to settle the dispute, so he did. He afterward revealed, 'I would not have yielded to the demand. But I did so because of the urgent requests of my people and my own strong desire to prevent bloodshed.'

The rainy season was well underway, and the next day they crossed two swollen rivers. After being in damp clothes the rest of that day and overnight, David became feverish. The dense forests through which they passed in the days that followed had many low-hanging vines which were up to three or four inches thick. Those riding on ox-back needed to quickly lift the vines over their heads or duck under them in order not to be dragged off their oxen.

One afternoon heavy rain made it difficult to see the low-hanging vines, and more than one rider was swept off the back of his ox. Livingstone had a stubborn, uncooperative ox named Sinbad that often gave him trouble. On this occasion Sinbad suddenly took off running through the forest. When David pulled back on the bridle to try to stop the galloping animal, the bridle broke and David fell to the ground, landing heavily on the top of his head. With his usual good humor, David related further, 'In addition, he gave me a kick on the thigh, clearly showing there is no love lost between us.'

Other tribes made unreasonable demands on Livingstone's company as they continued their journey, and eventually they found themselves with almost nothing of value left to trade. Early in April they came to the Quango River, which during that rainy season was a muddy, swollen river about 150 yards wide. They had nothing with which to hire boatmen to ferry them across.

Kimeya, the young leader of a small village nearby the Quango, told Livingstone, 'If you desire to cross the river rather than to turn back, you must give me a man, a tusk or an ox.' David sent back a message that all they had to offer in payment was a little meat and a few brass armlets. The brass rings actually belonged to a few of David's men, who took them off their arms and offered them as part of the needed payment.

Then, that same morning, as they waited to hear whether or not Kimeya would accept their offer, a young Portuguese military sergeant unexpectedly appeared at their camp. 'My name is Cypriano di Abreu,' he introduced himself to Livingstone. 'I am the commander of a Portuguese militia group stationed at a settlement three miles past the other side of the Quango. We have been placed at this outpost to ensure that Portuguese traders are able to freely operate in the region without being troubled by local tribes.'

'As I was passing by,' Cypriano continued, 'I thought I saw some of my countrymen being harassed by the natives. I find you are not Portuguese, but if you would like to, you're welcome to continue on with me. I'll make sure you get across the river safely into Portuguese territory. There you'll not be bothered by any more tribes.'

Livingstone's party quickly left their camp with Cypriano. When they reached the Quango, Cypriano assisted them in making arrangements with the boatmen to ferry them across the river. After crossing it, Cypriano then took them to the settlement of Ngango, where his small military force was stationed. There the sergeant and his friends treated Livingstone and his men with great kindness and provided them with many pumpkins and much manioc root for food.

Throughout the remainder of April and May, David's party traveled the final 360 miles to their destination of Loanda on Africa's west coast. They were treated with kindness and generosity by the governors of the Portuguese settlements on that final part of their journey. They were now in Angola, a region in southwest Africa that was governed by Portugal.

Unfortunately, Livingstone continued to suffer attacks of fever. At one point before they reached Loanda, a severe shivering fit left him insensible for several hours. They arrived at Loanda the last day of May. Since setting out from Sekeletu's town of Linyanti six months and three weeks earlier, they had traveled around 1,400 miles.

Trekking across the Continent

At Loanda Livingstone was warmly welcomed into the home of a British official named Edmund Gabriel. Portugal governed Angola, but for a dozen years the British Navy had patrolled the coastline of Angola to prevent slaves from being shipped from that country. Mr Gabriel was one of the British officials who helped stop the shipping of slaves there. When David's party arrived at Loanda, Gabriel provided each of the men with a new robe of striped cotton cloth and a red cap.

Livingstone started recovering his health, before suffering a severe relapse of both fever and diarrhea. 'I ate nothing during many days,' he later reported. 'I soon became reduced to a skeleton.' God in his mercy brought a British ship to Loanda just in time. With the skilled help of the ship's surgeon, David's suffering was relieved, and he again began to recover.

The ship's commander offered to take Livingstone back to England. The thought of being reunited with his family greatly appealed to him. He had been separated from them for over two years. However, he considered it his duty to get his men safely back to their own country in inner Africa. Having learned how difficult and dangerous it was to travel from Makolololand to the west coast, he thought he needed a simpler, safer route to the east coast.

On September 20, Livingstone's party left Loanda to begin their journey back to Makololo territory. The Portuguese Governor supplied each man with a suit of clothing, a white cotton blanket and a cap. He also sent several gifts for Chief Sekeletu. David provided each man with a musket for the return trip.

Time and again throughout the first seven months of this return journey Livingstone and his companions were attacked by fever. So many of David's men were laid low by fever at one Portuguese settlement that their entire party was delayed there for two months.

From mid-March to mid-April 1855 Livingstone suffered from rheumatic fever, which left him with a violent headache and much pain in his joints. For eight days he was confined to his small tent and was barely aware of what was happening around him.

At the small African village where David was recovering, a man in his party lost his temper while bargaining for a piece of meat with the village leader and struck him on the mouth. Livingstone left it to Pitsane, one of the Makololo leaders, to settle the dispute. After Pitsane gave a rifle and five generous portions of cloth to make amends for the offense, the chief suddenly demanded a cow as well. David was annoyed that so much had already been demanded from them and decided that no more would be given.

After Livingstone's company had left the village, the village leader and his men came rushing after them. They knocked to the ground the supplies which were carried by the men in the back of David's group. The members of the two opposing parties spread out behind the trees on both sides of the path. Several shots were fired from both sides, but thankfully no one was hurt.

Taking his revolver in his hand and momentarily forgetting about his fever, Livingstone staggered quickly along the path with two or three others. Fortunately, he soon met the chief. Wanting to bring the fighting to an immediate end but not actually intending to harm the village leader, David drew near to him and pointed his revolver at the man's stomach.

'Oh!' the chief cried out, 'I have only come to speak to you, and wish peace only.' Livingstone's men took the chief's rifle and found that he had fired it.

'We come only with peaceful intentions,' the village men insisted, seeing the danger their chief was in.

'But knocking our goods to the ground showed us the opposite,' David's companions stated.

'Let's all sit down and settle this amicably,' David said, and sat down himself. Pitsane did so also and placed his hand on David's revolver. This gesture calmed the villagers' fears, and they were seated as well.

'If you have truly come with peaceable intentions,' Livingstone told the chief, 'we have no other. Go away home to your village.'

After further discussion the two groups parted peacefully. David later commented: 'The villagers were no doubt pleased with being allowed to retreat unharmed. And we were also glad to get away without having shed a drop of blood.'

Livingstone's party revisited the Balonda villages, including Shinte's town, in June and July. They reached Barotse territory (the westernmost region under Makololo rule) toward the end of July. At the village of Libonta they were welcomed with great demonstrations of joy. The women came out to greet them with dancing and 'lullilooing', a joyous, high-pitched trilling sound they made with their tongues. Some rushed forward and kissed the hands and cheeks of Livingstone's men whom they knew.

'We were looked upon as men risen from the dead,' David afterward revealed. 'For the most skillful of their diviners had pronounced us to have perished long ago.' That Sunday, July 29, Livingstone led the village in having a day of thanksgiving to God for allowing their safe return. 'We have come,' David told the villagers, 'to thank God before all of you for His mercy in preserving us in dangers by strange tribes and sicknesses.'

One day as they continued down the Zambesi River in canoes, a hippopotamus suddenly rammed Livingstone's canoe with its head, nearly overturning the vessel. One of the Africans in the craft was pitched into the river by the force of the blow. Fortunately, they were near the riverbank, so David and the other seven men in the canoe were all able to spring safely to the shore. They saw the hippopotamus surface nearby, about ten yards out in the river. 'No damage was done,' David related, 'except a wetting of people and goods.'

Livingstone's company reached Sekeletu's town of Linyanti on September 11. Exactly twenty-two months had passed since they left Linyanti for the west coast in November 1853. And it had been almost a year since they left Loanda to return to Makololo territory.

David informed the Makololo of his desire to travel to the east coast to see if a better trade and supply route could be discovered from there than from the west coast. The Makololo agreed that he should follow the Zambesi River to find out if it could provide a reliable route to and from the east coast.

'Our ivory is at your disposal,' Sekeletu and his leaders told Livingstone. 'Take as much as you need for the coming journey. We trust your faithfulness to us, and that you will do your best to help us.'

When Livingstone set out from Linyanti on November 3, Sekeletu and 200 of his people accompanied him on the first leg of the journey. The chief provided David with twelve oxen and an abundant supply of corn and peanuts. He also gave him beads and hoes for trading with tribes along the way.

They first traveled by land north to Sesheke, an important Makololo town on the Zambesi River. (This was the location where Livingstone and Oswell had first seen the Zambesi over four years earlier.) From there David, Sekeletu and their companions set out downriver in canoes.

On November 16, they approached a gigantic waterfall that stretched across the Zambesi River. Livingstone had heard about it for several years, but neither he nor any other white man had ever seen it. The Makololo called it Mosioatunya, meaning 'smoke sounding'. The more ancient name for the falls was Shongwe, which meant 'the rainbow' or 'the place of the rainbow'. About six miles before reaching the falls, David observed five columns of vapor, colored white below and turning dark higher up, rising till they seemed to meet the clouds.

Further downriver Livingstone and several of his companions left their larger canoe and climbed into small, light vessels steered by local guides who were well acquainted with the rapids. They glided swiftly down to an island in the middle of the river. The island was perched on the northern edge of the precipice over which the water plunged with a roar.

They crept with awe to the edge of the waterfall and looked over it. The mighty Zambesi River was more than a mile wide at this location. It rushed past many small islands, thundered over the north wall of the falls, and fell more than 300 feet into a deep, narrow gorge below. There the water churned through the narrow channel until it rounded a corner and passed through an opening on the other side of the canyon wall.

In peering down into the chasm, Livingstone and his companions could see only a dense white cloud with two rainbows on it. The columns of water vapor that David had seen from six miles away rose some 250 feet into the air, then showered down on them, soon leaving their clothes and skin soaking wet.

Livingstone was the first white person ever to see the falls and was credited with being the first European to discover them. During his journeys he had thought about naming a significant geographical discovery in honor of Britain's Queen Victoria. He thought this magnificent waterfall was a worthy discovery with which to honor the Queen, so named it Victoria Falls.

After visiting the falls, Sekeletu departed with some of his men to return to Linyanti. He left 115 men to assist Livingstone. Fifteen large tusks and six or seven smaller ones were entrusted to the missionary. Some of the larger tusks weighed 100 or more pounds apiece.

From Victoria Falls Livingstone's company traveled northeast by land through the Batoka highlands in order to avoid tsetse flies which were known to be along that section of the Zambesi. As they trekked through the Batoka territory David concluded it would be a good location for a new missionary station. Stretching out along an extensive elevated plateau, the area did not have fever or tsetse. It offered rich soil for gardens and much pastureland for livestock. In addition, slave trading was not carried out in the Batoka region.

By the opening days of 1856 they made their way back to the Zambesi River. A month later they again left the Zambesi, this time to angle southeast of the river toward a Portuguese settlement named Tete. If they had followed the Zambesi as it made a large gradual bend east and then south, it would have led them to Tete. 'But the tribes there,' David had been warned, 'are unfriendly toward travelers and place heavy demands on them for permission to pass by their villages.'

Livingstone would later learn, after reaching Tete, of a reportedly 'small' rapids in the portion of the Zambesi River which he did not explore at this time, while still on his way to Tete. The rapids, located a number of miles upriver from Tete, were called Kebrabasa. It was described simply as being a collection of rocks that jutted out across the Zambesi. David had no way of knowing that his decision not to examine that part of the Zambesi at this time would create considerable difficulties for him in later years.

They reached Tete on March 2. It was the westernmost Portuguese settlement on the Zambesi. In the past Tete and the surrounding area had been a strong trading district which exported large amounts of grain, coffee, sugar, oil, cotton, indigo and ivory. But in more recent years, the slave trade had swept through the region. The slave trade tempted people with higher profits that could be gained more quickly. It destroyed the other forms of beneficial trade and robbed the area of its workers, as many of those laborers were taken from the country as slaves.

Livingstone and thirty-two men left Tete on April 22 to continue downriver toward the coast. He had not experienced any fever during the four months he traveled from Sekeletu's town to Tete. However, beginning at Tete and continuing throughout the remainder of his journey to the coast he again suffered repeated attacks of fever.

Along the way they passed the Shire River, a large tributary that flowed into the Zambesi from the north. Several miles past the Shire, the Zambesi left the hill country and flowed southeast through a long, broad flatland area to the Indian Ocean. There where the Zambesi turned south and east, the small Mutu River flowed in a more eastward direction for some seventy miles to the town of Quilimane on the coast. David's party followed the Mutu, arriving at Quilimane on May 20. It had taken them six and a half months to travel the 1,000 miles from Linyanti to this coastal destination.

When Livingstone reached Quilimane, he became the first person ever to have crossed the African continent from one coast to the other. He felt privileged to have succeeded in doing that. Yet, as noteworthy as that accomplishment was, he viewed it only as the first step toward a far more important goal: He had pioneered a route by which Christian missionary work could be brought to the regions through which he had traveled. In expressing this, David recorded in a letter what became one of the most famous statements he ever made: 'The end of the geographical feat is but the beginning of the missionary enterprise.'

Some letters were waiting for Livingstone when he arrived in Quilimane, but he was disappointed that none of them were from his family members. Four long years had passed since his wife and children sailed back to Britain from Cape Town. He had regularly written to his family, and they had often written him throughout those years. However, with no reliable postal service in the interior of Africa, it took many months for letters to pass between Britain and inner Africa. As a result, in all the time David had been apart from his family, he had received only one letter from Mary, and that one not until some three years after she wrote it!

At the beginning of June, Livingstone told the Makololo who had traveled with him to Quilimane: 'I am sending you back to your countrymen who stayed behind at Tete. I have traded ten of the tusks we brought with us for a generous supply of brass wire and calico cloth. These are for all of you who have served with me, including those back in Tete. I plan to pay a brief visit to my home country, then return to Quilimane in less than a year. I will then come to Tete and take you safely back to Chief Sekeletu.'

Livingstone left Quilimane to begin a long journey to Britain on July 12. He arrived in London, England, on December 9. Sixteen years and one day had passed since he first sailed from London aboard the *George* to go to Africa as a missionary.

Leading the Zambesi Expedition

David was joyfully welcomed back home by Mary and
their four children. Robert, Agnes, Thomas and Oswell
were now ten, nine, seven and five years of age. They
had all grown and changed a great deal in the four and
a half years since their father last saw them in Africa.

All of Britain welcomed Livingstone back as
something of a national hero. The Royal Geographical
Society (RGS) held a special meeting on December 15,
just six days after his arrival back in England, to
welcome and honor him. He was awarded the RGS's
Patron's Gold Medal (more commonly called the
Queen's Gold Medal) for his widespread explorations
in Africa.

The following day the London Missionary Society
(LMS) held a public reception for Livingstone.
'Through David Livingstone's tireless, selfless
efforts,' one LMS Director stated, 'the door has been
opened for the Christian Gospel to be brought to
many tribes who have never before heard the joyous
message of salvation.' The Director rightly added: 'In

speaking so highly of Mr Livingstone's service of the Lord Jesus, we ultimately give God all the glory for his work in and through his devoted servant.'

Lord Shaftesbury, the prominent Christian politician and social reformer who led the meeting, praised Mary as well: 'Mrs Livingstone has faithfully supported her husband in his missionary endeavors and certainly deserves a portion of the credit for his successes. She has shared not a little in hardships and personal sacrifices. All this she did in order to help bring Christianity to Africa.'

Livingstone was strongly encouraged to write a book about his travels and discoveries in Africa. He did so while living with his family in London the first several months of 1857. He often worked on his book with his children playing noisily around him.

Sometimes he took time off from his writing to go on walks with his children. Along the way he would suddenly disappear into the nearby forest, leading the children to go looking for him. Then just as suddenly he would reappear from some unexpected corner of the wood, to the surprise and delight of his children.

Livingstone had become so famous that if he went out on busy London streets he quickly attracted a mob of people eager to see or meet him. He once entered a church with his head down and sat in a shadowed pew under the balcony, in an effort not to be noticed. However, the preacher caught sight of him and, in his closing prayer, drew attention to

Livingstone's presence. As a result, immediately after the service many people came rushing toward the missionary. Some even climbed over pews in their eagerness to see him and shake his hand!

David finished writing his book *Missionary Travels and Researches in South Africa* that July. When it was published in November it ended up being 687 pages long! It is quite remarkable that it took him only six months to write such a long book. *Missionary Travels* was so popular it went on to sell 70,000 copies. In that day if a volume sold 10,000 copies it was considered a great success.

Originally Livingstone had planned to return to Africa that April to take the men from Tete back to Chief Sekeletu. However, David received promises from government officials in Portugal that they would send out instructions for Portuguese governors in the Zambesi River region to take care of his men until he was able to return to them. Being confident that his African companions would be well cared for, David was able to stay longer in Britain, finishing his book then traveling around to promote interest in his future work in Africa.

At the beginning of 1857 Livingstone had been invited by the London Missionary Society to take the lead in establishing a new mission station among the Makololo when he returned to Africa. David knew, though, that other LMS missionaries were available to do that, so he declined the invitation. He instead accepted an offer from the British Government to become the leader of the Zambesi Expedition.

The purposes of the Zambesi Expedition were to explore the Zambesi River and its tributaries, and to determine if trading opportunities could be established with the tribes that lived in those areas. In this way not only *commerce* (beneficial trading opportunities) but also *Christianity* could be brought to that broad region of Africa. In addition, other *civilizing influences* like education, health care and peace between tribes could be introduced. It was thought that Christianity, commerce and civilization would bring an end to slavery all across southern Africa. Britain would also benefit from this by establishing profitable trade with many African tribes.

Some people criticized Livingstone for deciding to lead the Zambesi Expedition, saying that he was forsaking God's call on his life to be a missionary. But throughout all his years of service in Africa, David always viewed himself first and foremost as a missionary. So now he viewed his leadership of the Zambesi Expedition as an opportunity to carry out a much larger vision that he had come to have for the far greater good of Africa.

David's efforts would open the door for tremendous benefits to be brought to numerous tribes throughout a vast region of Africa. He certainly did not think that he would accomplish all or even most of those results on his own. Rather, he would merely get the good work started. Others would follow him into the areas he had pioneered and would bring immeasurable good to innumerable people.

After finishing the writing of *Missionary Travels*, Livingstone traveled throughout England, Scotland and Ireland. He was invited to speak in many cities and towns, at the meetings of scientific and commercial organizations, at Oxford and Cambridge Universities, as well as at churches.

He received a number of gifts and honors. Some cities presented him with generous financial gifts, which were partly intended to help care for his family's material and educational needs. Oxford University and Glasgow University conferred honorary doctoral degrees on him. He was even honored with an interview with Queen Victoria who was deeply interested in his work and discoveries in Africa. The Queen was then thirty-eight years old, nearly seven years younger than Livingstone.

The missionary's good sense of humor shone through during that interview. 'I will now be able to inform the African peoples that I have seen my chief,' he told the Queen. 'My inability to do so before has always greatly surprised them.' Queen Victoria laughed heartily when he further informed her: 'The Africans have often asked me if my chief were wealthy. When I assure them she is very wealthy, they ask me how many cows she has!'

When it came time for the Zambesi Expedition to leave for Africa on March 10, 1858, David and Mary took with them only their youngest son, Oswell, then seven years of age. They left Robert, Agnes and Thomas in Britain to continue their education there. Many missionary families in that era sent their children back to their home country to be educated while the parents continued carrying out their missionary service. Often loving family members or friends of the missionaries would help care for the children during those years of being separated from their parents.

During the years that David was apart from his children, he regularly wrote them letters. In those letters he shared news about his activities in Africa that he thought would be of interest to them. He also gave his loving, fatherly advice and encouragement about their relationship with the Lord Jesus, their service of God, their education, their physical health, and other important topics.

While on their way to Africa, David and Mary realized that she was expecting another child. The expedition was to begin where the Zambesi River flowed into the Indian Ocean on Africa's southeast coast. Fever was common in that coastal region. David and Mary decided that she should go to her parents' home at Kuruman to give birth. Mary, Oswell and the baby could join David somewhere further up the Zambesi after he was out of the fever district. The Zambesi Expedition reached Cape Town on April 21. Ten days later David and Mary experienced a very sad and painful parting when the expedition continued on to the Zambesi without her.

Besides Livingstone as leader of the expedition, the Zambesi Expedition initially had six other British members: a navigator to guide their steamship; an engineer to keep the boat in good repair; a mining geologist to study the minerals of the country; a botanist to study Africa's plants; an artist and storekeeper of their food and other supplies; David's younger brother Charles who was to serve as the Doctor's General Assistant and as the Moral Agent to encourage the expedition's spiritual emphases. Charles, who had spent several years in America attending college and seminary then, serving as a pastor, had recently returned to assist David in the expedition. In addition, ten Kroomen were hired at Sierra Leone (on the northwest coast of Africa), when the expedition was on its way to southern Africa. The Kroomen were African sailors who carried out much of the expedition's physical work.

Before leaving England, a modest paddlewheel steamship had been purchased by the British Government for use in the Zambesi Expedition. It was named the *Ma Robert*, the African name for Mary Livingstone. The vessel was seventy-five feet long by eight feet wide and sat two feet deep in the water. (That depth was the steamship's 'draft.') It had a woodburning furnace to produce steam power to turn the ship's paddlewheel, two sails for wind power, and a twelve-horsepower engine for additional power if needed. The bottom and sides of the vessel were built of a new, untried type of steel that was very thin and would later prove to be a problem.

A large British ship named the *Pearl* carried the Zambesi Expedition members, their supplies and equipment, as well as the sections of the *Ma Robert* from England to one of the four mouths of the Zambesi River at the Indian Ocean. After arriving at the Zambesi the middle of May, the pieces of the *Ma Robert* were bolted back together.

After the *Pearl* left, the expedition needed to transport its 25,000 tons of supplies up the river using the *Ma Robert*. The small steamer could carry only a few tons of supplies at a time. They needed to make several trips to move their goods from one place to another further up the river, which took a lot of time. Their progress was also slowed by the fact that an immense amount of wood was needed to produce steam power for the *Ma Robert*. They ended up spending almost as much time cutting wood along the way as they did making progress up the river.

Before the Zambesi Expedition left the coast on June 10, Livingstone had learned that a murderous, slave-trading tribal leader who lived near the confluence of the Zambesi and Shire Rivers was leading a rebellion against the Portuguese in that vicinity. Now on July 21, Livingstone and his company stopped near Mazaro to cut wood for the *Ma Robert*. Mazaro was located not far from the Mutu River, which David had followed eastward to Quilimane in 1856.

A thick fog that morning prevented Livingstone's party from seeing that fierce fighting had already taken place that day between Portuguese soldiers and rebel African tribesmen. When Livingstone and his companions arrived at Mazaro during a lull in the battle they were shocked and sickened to find dead bodies, some of them headless, lying along the shoreline.

Portuguese military officers came out to Livingstone. 'Governor da Silva has come from Quilimane to lead our forces,' they informed David. 'He is here but is seriously ill with fever. Will you please take him across to Shupanga on the other side of the river?'

'Yes, I will be happy to do so,' David replied.

Just then rifle balls began to whistle around in all directions as the fighting resumed. Livingstone went to the hut where Governor da Silva lay gravely ill. Livingstone sent one of the expedition officers to have the Kroomen from the *Ma Robert* carry the governor back to the steamship. However, the frightened officer failed to carry out that order, so no one came from the vessel.

Unable to find another man to help him take the governor to the ship, Livingstone managed to get da Silva to his feet. The governor was much taller than

David and swayed back and forth due to his weakness. He leaned heavily on the missionary, and only with difficulty could David support his weight. As they staggered along unevenly, they looked like one drunken man helping another. At last, a Portuguese sergeant came to aid Livingstone in getting da Silva to the boat, so they were able to transport the governor to safety at Shupanga.

The Zambesi Expedition finally reached Tete on September 8. It had taken them nearly three months to travel the 260 miles from the ocean to Tete. In addition, two years, four and a half months had passed since Livingstone left his men at Tete in 1856 with the assurance that he would go to Britain then return in about a year to take them back to Sekeletu.

As soon as David went ashore, he was surrounded by his faithful Makololo. They eagerly grasped his hands and arms and lullilooed with joy. Some began to hug him, but one of them called out, 'Don't do that! You will make his clothes dirty!' David was usually reserved about showing emotion, and almost never wept. However, later he recounted: 'It is not often I have shed a tear, but they came in spite of my efforts to hold them back.'

Livingstone was terribly sad to learn that thirty Makololo had died when a smallpox epidemic came to Tete. He was even more troubled to learn that six of their young men had been murdered when they tried to pay a friendly visit to a neighboring chief.

The chief was drunk and suspicious that they had come to bewitch him, so ordered them to be killed.

During November and December the Zambesi Expedition made two explorations of the Kebrabasa Gorge upriver from Tete. Livingstone had been told a little about Kebrabasa but had not seen it during his transcontinental journey in 1856. At that time Kebrabasa was described to him as a small rapids and a collection of rocks jutting out across the Zambesi.

However, now at the end of 1858, as David and his fellow travelers explored about thirty miles of Kebrabasa, they found it to be a long, deep, dangerous gorge where the Zambesi squeezed and rushed through a series of tall canyon walls and high hills. They had to carry out most of the exploratory journey on foot, because in many places the *Ma Robert* could not have passed safely through the rocky rapids or the towering rock walls of the narrow canyons.

Only with the greatest difficulty could Livingstone and a few men make their way around the gigantic boulders and along the steep canyon walls which they encountered. Most of the men found the journey too hard to continue, and David allowed them to stay behind until he and a few others returned from going further upriver.

At the most westerly point which a few of them reached, they discovered a waterfall which was more than fifty yards wide and about thirty feet high. Judging from high-water marks which he could see on the rock canyon walls at that location, Livingstone thought that the river must rise about eighty vertical feet higher than its current level when it was flooding.

At this time late in the year the river was at a low level. David speculated that when the river was overflowing this waterfall and other dangerous points in the gorge would likely be submerged and eliminated. Then a boat with a strong engine should be able to pass safely upstream through the gorge. However, Livingstone had to admit to himself that he really had no way of knowing if boats would be able to pass through the Kebrabasa Gorge during a certain period of the year. In the end he seems to have concluded that it would probably not work out.

This meant that the Zambesi River would not provide a highway which missionaries and traders could use to bring Christianity and commerce into the interior of southcentral Africa. Despite this disappointing realization, David did not give up on his dreams for the good of Africa. Instead, he started looking for some other area in Africa where those dreams could still be fulfilled.

New Explorations and Fulfilling a Promise

Throughout the following year, 1859, Livingstone and his fellow explorers, including some of the Makololo, made three explorations up the Shire River which flowed into the Zambesi from the north. During the opening days of January they traveled 100 miles 'as the crow flies' up the Shire River in the *Ma Robert*. David estimated they actually traveled twice that distance by following all the curves in the Shire.

The Portuguese did not risk traveling up the Shire because they believed the Manganja people who lived there were bloodthirsty savages. More than once Livingstone's party was confronted by hundreds of tribesmen armed with bows and poisoned arrows. David greeted them in cordial fashion, then explained: 'We are Englishmen who have come neither to take slaves nor to fight. Rather, we wish to open a path by which our countrymen might follow us, to purchase your cotton or whatever else you might have to sell, except slaves.' After learning that, the Manganja tribesmen quickly became more friendly.

The furthest up the Shire River Livingstone's company got during that first exploration was Mamvira. Mamvira was the first in a series of six large waterfalls in a thirty-three mile stretch of the Shire River as it continued in a northeast direction. Livingstone named this group of waterfalls the Murchison Cataracts in honor of Sir Roderick Murchison, the President of Britain's Royal Geographical Society and a supportive friend to David.

During March and April, Livingstone's party made a second journey up the Shire. This time they left the *Ma Robert* at a village named Chibisa, ten miles below the waterfall at Mamvira. Continuing on foot to the north and east, they walked through the mountainous Shire highlands region for two weeks. On April 18, Livingstone and his companions discovered Lake Shirwa, which David estimated to be sixty or eighty miles long (north to south) and about twenty miles broad. They were intrigued when the people who lived in that area told them that Lake Shirwa was nothing in size compared to a much larger lake located further north.

A few months later they made a third exploration up the Shire, this time into the upper Shire River region north of the Murchison Cataracts. On September 16, Livingstone's expedition discovered the much larger body of water – Lake Nyassa (modern Lake Malawi) – which they had earlier heard about. They had arrived at the southeastern tip but, due to grassfires in the area, they were unable to see many miles up the lake's shores.

They had no way of knowing that they were, in fact, looking out over the southernmost portion of the ninth largest lake in the world and the third biggest in Africa! Lake Nyassa measures 350 miles long and 47 miles at its widest point. It is also extremely deep, with an average depth of 958 feet.

While spending the night near the spot where the Shire River flowed out of Lake Nyassa, they were visited by six members of a large Arab slave party that was camped close by. The slave traders carried long muskets and looked like villains to David and his men. 'We have several young children we can sell you,' the slavers offered.

'We are Englishmen,' Livingstone responded. 'We do not buy or sell slaves. And neither should you. What you are doing is very bad.'

When the slave traders heard that they were Englishmen, they looked frightened and quickly left. That same night the traders left the place where they were camped and moved on toward the coast where they would sell their slaves.

After returning to the Zambesi River in early November, David received a letter from his wife Mary, informing him of the birth of their daughter Anna Mary. She had been born in Kuruman nearly a year earlier, on November 16, 1858. This was the first time David received news of the baby's birth.

After giving birth to Anna Mary, it was still not at all clear when and where Mary Livingstone would be able to rejoin her husband. She decided it would be best to return to Britain to care for her children there until the future became clearer. After sailing back to Britain with Oswell and Anna Mary in the opening months of 1859, she settled with her children in Glasgow.

In the middle of May of the following year, 1860, David set out from Tete with Sekeletu's men to return them to their chief. Charles Livingstone and John Kirk, the expedition's botanist, went with them. The *Ma Robert* was left at Tete, and the journey was carried out on foot.

One day in early July, while walking through a thick, thorny jungle, Livingstone got separated from the others in his group. As David stooped over to pick up a piece of wild fruit, a rhinoceros suddenly appeared, snorted angrily and charged toward him. The animal, when less than its own body-length away from Livingstone, stopped for no apparent reason and stood completely still, as if it had been turned into stone.

This gave David the opportunity to escape. As he fled, a branch snagged his pocket watch. Turning halfway around to grab the watch, Livingstone caught a glance of the cow and her calf still standing on the exact same spot, 'as if stopped in the middle of her charge by an unseen hand'. No doubt it was God's protective hand that stopped and held the beast for a time!

After Livingstone had gotten about fifty yards away from the rhinos, and thinking his companions were close behind him, he shouted, 'Look out there!'

At the sound of his voice the mother rhino rushed off in another direction, snorting loudly. David usually traveled unarmed before this incident, but never afterward.

They learned that Sekeletu was currently residing at Sesheke on the Zambesi River rather than at Linyanti. When Livingstone's party reached Sesheke in mid-August, they found Sekeletu living by himself because he thought he had leprosy. Livingstone and John Kirk, who was also a medical doctor, visited Sekeletu and treated his skin disease. They determined it was not leprosy but a less-serious condition that caused blisters and sores to form on his skin. Through those treatments the chief's skin condition started clearing up nicely.

Livingstone's company, which again included a number of Makololo, left Sesheke on September 17. Sekeletu's men were sent to assist David in going back down the Zambesi River, this time in canoes. The chief's men were also to see if the canoes could travel safely through the Kebrabasa Gorge, then to bring back medicine to help treat Sekeletu's skin disease.

When they reached the western end of Kebrabasa Gorge on November 12, they were able to glide swiftly through it for a few miles. Then, however, the river rushed into a narrower passage with many waterfalls. A couple of their canoes passed safely down a narrow channel that was split in two by a collection of rocks.

At the base of those rocks, a deep ugly whirlpool alternately opened and closed. As Livingstone's canoe came near it, the vessel seemed to be drifting broadside into the whirlpool, despite the frantic efforts of the paddlers to avoid it. The men in the other canoes saw what was happening and cried out, 'Look where these people are going! Look, look!'

Just then a loud crash was heard as Kirk's canoe dashed against a rock that stuck out into the churning river. Kirk pulled himself onto the ledge. A couple of the Africans, while holding on to the rocks, managed to save the canoe. David's canoe, meanwhile, was saved when the frightful dark hole in the whirlpool closed just before the vessel passed over top of it.

Thankfully, no lives were lost in this threatening incident, but Kirk lost everything of value in his canoe. Those items included two scientific instruments, his clothes, some handwritten notes he had kept during that journey, and his botanical drawings of about 100 fruit trees he had found in the interior of Africa.

Leaving their canoes behind, they continued the downriver journey on foot. They passed two large trading parties from Tete that were headed upriver. The traders were leading a number of Manganja women from the Shire River region who were to be sold for ivory. Each of the women had a rope tied around her neck, and all of them were fastened to one long rope.

Interfering with the Slave Trade

When Livingstone reached Tete on November 23, he was delighted to learn that the British Government had agreed to his repeated requests that a new steamship be sent out for their use in continuing the Zambesi Expedition. That vessel, named the *Pioneer*, was already on its way to the mouth of the Zambesi.

Livingstone was also highly pleased to learn that a group of missionaries was to arrive at the same time as the *Pioneer*. The missionaries were part of the new Universities Mission (UM) and planned to establish a mission station somewhere in the Shire River region. The UM was made up of men from Oxford, Cambridge and Dublin Universities who belonged to the Church of England. Livingstone had special interest in this new mission, which had formed in response to his visits to Oxford, Cambridge and Dublin in 1857-1858.

For well over a year, holes had been developing in the thin metal plates on the bottom of the *Ma Robert*. The steel plates were so thin and fragile that the leaks could not be fixed by bolting or hammering new pieces of metal to them. The only way to patch the holes was to cover them using canvas bags filled with clay.

As Livingstone's company continued down the Zambesi that December, new leaks developed every day, and the steamer's three main compartments filled with water at night. At last the vessel ran aground on a sandbank and could not be gotten off it. The craft slowly filled with water, and they had to remove all their belongings from it. The river rose during the night and covered the boat. All that could be seen of the *Ma Robert* the next morning was the top six feet of her two masts that held the ship's sails.

Using canoes, they were able to reach Kongone Harbor at one of the mouths of the Zambesi River on January 4, 1861. There for a month they endured clouds of mosquitoes, much fever, high winds and heavy rains. Their food supply ran out, leaving them with only coarse African porridge to eat. The *Pioneer* did not arrive and enter the harbor until early February.

The *Pioneer* was a good-sized, steam-powered paddleboat that also had several sails for wind power. It was 115 feet long, forty feet longer than the *Ma Robert*. But the *Pioneeer's* draft (depth in the water) of five feet would prove to be a problem in maneuvering it through the Zambesi and Shire Rivers when those were at lower levels. In addition to the steamship itself, ten British men with a variety of skills had been sent out to assist with the Zambesi Expedition.

The members of the new Universities Mission (UM) arrived in a different ship around that same time. The UM was led by thirty-five-year-old William Mackenzie, a Church of England bishop. The rest of the UM party consisted of six British missionaries and five Africans who had come from Cape Colony to assist them.

The *Pioneer*, carrying the men of the Zambesi Expedition and the Universities Mission, made its way slowly up the Zambesi and Shire Rivers. It needed to stop frequently so wood could be cut with which to fuel the vessel. Because of the *Pioneer's* deep draft, it repeatedly had to be freed from or even dragged over sandbars. The paddlewheel and other parts of the steamer were sometimes damaged and needed to be repaired.

At last, on July 8 they reached the village of Chibisa, which Livingstone's company had visited on its earlier explorations up the Shire River region. One week later David, the Bishop, and a combined group of their men went out to explore the Shire highlands. They desired to find a location where the UM could establish a missionary station.

When they arrived at the village of a chief named Mbame, he told them that a slave party on its way to Tete would soon pass through his village with their captives. 'Shall we interfere with what the slave traders are doing?' Livingstone asked his companions. They concluded that the time had come to do so.

A few minutes later a long line of eighty-four bound slaves, most of them women and children, came wending their way into the valley where Mbame's village was located. Slave drivers, armed with muskets, marched along confidently in the front, middle and rear of the procession. Some of them announced their approach to the village by blowing triumphantly on long tin horns. However, the instant the slave drivers saw the Englishmen, they quickly ran away into the forest.

Only the leader of the slave party at the head of the procession remained, and that was because a Makololo had taken a tight grip on his hand and would not let him go. He turned out to be a well-known slave of Major Sicard in Tete named Katura. Katura claimed that he had purchased these slaves. However, all but four of the captives revealed that they had been seized in war. Several of the women had been captured after their husbands were killed. While Livingstone was asking the slaves questions, Katura managed to escape.

The captives knelt down and, as a sign of their thanks to those who were freeing them, energetically clapped their hands. Livingstone's associates used their knives to cut away the ropes that bound the women and children. A saw that Bishop Mackenzie had in his baggage was used to free the captured men from the thick slave sticks that had been fastened around their necks. The freed women were promptly clothed with calico cloth.

The previous day the murderous slave drivers had shot two women for attempting to untie the cords that bound them. The slavers did this as a warning to the others not to try to escape. A man was also killed after he became too exhausted to carry a load.

'All of you are free to go wherever you please,' Livingstone informed the eighty-four former captives. 'You are no longer slaves. Or if you choose to, you may remain with those who have set you free. We will feed and protect you.'

All the freed people chose to stay. Bishop Mackenzie immediately took them into his mission work, to be educated as members of a Christian community.

Three days later, a Friday, Livingstone and Mackenzie visited the village of Chigunda, a prominent Manganja chief in the area. When Chigunda learned that Mackenzie and the freed slaves planned to settle and raise crops somewhere in the highlands country, the chief immediately invited the Bishop to come and live with him at a nearby location named Magomero. 'There is room enough for both of us there,' Chigunda told Mackenzie. Magomero was located some sixty miles northeast of the village of Chibisa on the Shire River.

The following Monday, Livingstone's company freed forty-three more slaves. That entire group of captives had been totally naked, so David provided all of them with cloth for clothing.

The next day Livingstone, Mackenzie and their expedition heard that a group of African tribesmen called the Ajawa were burning a village just a few miles away. The Ajawa had been attacking and plundering

Manganja villages in that area for about three months. They sold the slaves whom they captured in those raids to Portuguese slave traders.

Livingstone hoped to have a peaceful visit with the Ajawa. That afternoon they saw the smoke of burning villages. Then they spotted a long line of Ajawa warriors, with their captives, coming around the hillside toward them.

'We come in peace,' Livingstone called out to the Ajawa. 'We just want to talk with you.'

But the Ajawa ran off yelling, 'War! War!' Some of the Manganja captives threw down the loads they had been carrying and fled to the hills, thus escaping from their captors.

A large group of armed men came running up from a nearby Ajawa village and quickly surrounded Livingstone's party. The Ajawa hid behind rocks and in the long grass. 'We have come to talk rather than to fight,' David again called out.

The Ajawa, however, did not believe this and began to shoot at the expedition with their poisoned arrows. One of David's men was wounded through the arm. Four of the Ajawa had muskets and started firing at them with those. This led some of Livingstone's group to shoot back in self-defense. When the Ajawa realized that their opponents' rifles could shoot much further than their bows and muskets, they stopped fighting and retreated.

Livingstone had no intention of fighting the Ajawa when they went to visit them. In fact, because they did not plan to even hunt in the area, each man had only one bullet in his rifle. David had not even brought his rifle or pistol.

After this conflict Livingstone commented: 'Though we could not blame ourselves for the actions we had taken, we felt sorry for what had happened. It was the first time we had ever been attacked by the natives or come into collision with them. Had we known better the effect of slavery and murder on the temper of these bloodthirsty marauders, we should have tried sending messages and presents before going near them.'

From early August to early November, Livingstone and two dozen of the company returned to Lake Nyassa. They took with them a light, narrow rowboat (called a gig) with four oars. They hired people along the way to carry the gig around the Murchison Cataracts, then used the vessel to proceed up the broad, deep waters of the upper Shire River and along the western side of Lake Nyassa.

Strong winds often came down from the high hills and tall mountains that stood beside Lake Nyassa, stirring up tremendous storms on the lake. One day Livingstone and some of his companions found themselves about a mile out on the lake, trapped for six hours between tall, powerful waves that threatened to sink their boat. They knew that if they tried to land the gig, the rough surf along the shore would break the vessel into pieces.

Several of David's fellow travelers and some local Africans stood on the high cliffs overlooking the lake. As the large waves repeatedly seemed to swallow up the small boat, they cried out, 'They are lost! They are all dead!' When the storm finally subsided and David and his companions were able to return safely to shore, the other members of their party welcomed them warmly, as one does with a good friend after being separated for a long time.

Near one of the places where slaves were transported across Lake Nyassa, Livingstone and his British associates were robbed one night as they slept. This was the first time that had ever happened to Livingstone in all the years he had been in Africa.

Waking up the next morning, someone exclaimed, 'My bag is gone – with all my clothes and my boots too!'

'And mine!' stated another.

'And mine also,' added yet another, 'with the bag of beads and the rice!'

'Is the cloth taken?' one anxiously asked. For if that had been stolen, it would have been the same as losing all their money, since cloth was what they used for trading.

'No,' answered another. 'I used that as my pillow last night, so it is safe.'

Livingstone had two pairs of pants, a shirt and some rifle balls stolen from him. Kirk and Charles lost clothes, including boots. One man had slept in his best suit that night, thus saving it from being stolen. Fortunately, the thieves did not steal the rifles or pistols. David and his companions needed to sew new clothes for themselves.

As they continued exploring the western side of Lake Nyassa, they found that a fierce tribe named the Mazitu had recently attacked villages along the northern end of the lake. The Mazitu lived in the highlands to the west of Lake Nyassa. They had large herds of cattle and sometimes carried out raids against other tribes in the area. The Mazitu killed, plundered and carried off as captives only boys and girls around ten years of age. David's company saw burned villages near the shoreline. Corpses of those who had been killed by the Mazitu not many weeks before lay around on the ground.

Livingstone had earlier learned that each year 19,000 Africans were taken from the Lake Nyassa region to be sold as slaves in the large Arab slave market on the island of Zanzibar, off the southeast coast of Africa. That number did not include those African slaves who were shipped from Portuguese ports on Africa's east coast. Based on what he had seen in recent months, David now estimated that many thousands of additional Africans died every year as a result of the slave trade. Many were killed in the fighting that took place during slave raids; others perished from ill treatment at the hands of slavedrivers; still more died as a result of famine which frequently followed slave forays.

Sad Deaths and Destruction

In mid-November, after returning from Lake Nyassa, the members of the Zambesi Expedition set out for the coast in the *Pioneer*. A ship was expected there the following month that was to bring Mary Livingstone back to David as well as several new members to join the Universities Mission.

The ship would also bring another smaller steamer, the *Lady Nyassa*, which the Zambesi Expedition would use in fulfilling some of its explorations on the lake for which it was named. Livingstone had not asked the British Government to supply him with this steamer, perhaps thinking they would turn down his request or would take too long in granting it. Instead, he ordered the *Lady Nyassa* on his own, and planned to pay for the vessel himself.

The Shire River was at a low water level at that time of year. Just twenty miles south of the village of Chibisa, the *Pioneer* ran aground in shallow water, and there it remained stuck for five 'weary' weeks! Sadly, while they were forced to wait there, the carpenter's mate, a seemingly healthy young man, was seized with fever and died just one day later. He was the first British member of the Zambesi Expedition to die but not the last.

The *Pioneer* was at last able to make its way down the Shire and the Zambesi, reaching the coast on January 23, 1862. Eight days later a British military ship named the *Gorgon* arrived offshore. It was towing another ship, the *Hetty Ellen*, which brought Mary Livingstone, the additional six members of the Universities Mission, and the twenty-four sections of the *Lady Nyassa*.

David and Mary Livingstone were joyfully reunited on February 1. Since their painful parting at Cape Town in May of 1858, they had been separated for more than three and a half years.

Captain John Wilson of the *Gorgon*, along with fifty of his men and two large paddle box boats from his ship, accompanied the *Pioneer* when it headed back up the Zambesi on February 10. The main purpose of Captain Wilson's men and boats going with Livingstone for a time was to assist in moving the heavily laden *Pioneer,* along with the many tons of ironwork of the *Lady Nyassa*, up the Zambesi toward the Shire.

One week later, Captain Wilson, seven of his men, and two new members of the Universities Mission, along with John Kirk to act as their guide, boarded a smaller whaler boat and set off more quickly upriver. Their purpose was to meet Bishop Mackenzie at the mouth of the Ruo River, where it emptied into the Shire

River from the east. As had earlier been agreed upon, it was anticipated that the Bishop would be waiting there for the new members of his mission.

Tragically, when Wilson's party made their way first to the mouth of the Ruo, then further upriver to the village of Chibisa, they were shocked to learn that Bishop Mackenzie had died of fever at the Ruo on January 31. In addition, Henry Burrup, another leader of the Universities Mission, had died of disease at the UM mission station of Magomero two weeks after the bishop's death.

When the *Pioneer* reached Shupanga at the end of February, Livingstone's company began assembling the *Lady Nyassa* on the edge of the Zambesi River. David and Mary set up a tent nearby, overlooking the river, in which they lived. Captain Wilson, his men and paddle box boats returned to the mouth of the Zambesi, from which the *Gorgon* steamed to Cape Town.

Several of Livingstone's men were suffering from fever and dysentery. Mary began having frequent attacks of fever, but they lasted only a few hours. At first this caused no alarm, as many members of the Zambesi Expedition suffered from fever, and normally that could be effectively treated with medicine.

However, on April 21, Mary had a severe attack of fever. In the days that followed, her stomach would not accept any food or medicine, so she was unable to be helped by normal treatments. She was moved into a large stone home called the Shupanga House, which was located about 100 yards up a gently sloping hill from the Zambesi River.

Despite the diligent efforts of both Doctor Livingstone and Doctor Kirk to treat Mary, she died as the sun was setting on Sunday, April 27. She was only forty-one years old at the time of her death. The next day her body was buried under the branches of a large baobab tree that grew not far from the Shupanga House.

While David was comforted to know that Mary was now safely with the Lord in heaven, he was still extremely saddened at the death of his wife whom he had deeply loved. Around that time, he wrote in his private journal: 'I wept over her who well deserved many tears. I loved her when I married her, and the longer I lived with her I loved her the more. God pity our poor children who were all tenderly attached to her.'

Several days later David wrote to a friend about Mary's death: 'With a sore and heavy heart I have to tell of the death of my dear bosom friend of eighteen years. I cannot tell you how greatly I feel the loss. It feels as if heart and strength were taken out of me – my future is all dark.'

Despite his deep sorrow, Livingstone needed to press on in leading the Zambesi Expedition. Construction work on the *Lady Nyassa* was finished in late June. By then, however, water levels in the Zambesi and Shire had fallen so low that it was thought impossible to transport the two steamships upriver to the Murchison Cataracts until the heavy seasonal rains came in December.

As a result, early in August, Livingstone and his men instead sailed down the Zambesi to the coast, then several hundred miles up around the southeastern side of Africa to where the Rovuma River flowed into the Indian Ocean. 'The headwaters of the Rovuma are said to be located not too far east of Lake Nyassa,' David reflected. 'I desire to learn if the Rovuma might provide a shorter and simpler water route to Lake Nyassa than the Zambesi and Shire do. I also want to see if profitable trade can be promoted in the Rovuma region, and if the area is healthy enough for missionaries to settle and minister there.'

Using smaller boats, Livingstone's company spent one month exploring the Rovuma. The results were not encouraging. Rocky rapids stopped their progress when they were still many miles from Lake Nyassa. As happened with the Zambesi and Shire Rivers, so also the water level of the Rovuma dropped sharply at certain times of the year, making it unreliable for travel during those periods. The Rovuma region did not seem overly healthy, as a few of the expedition members developed fever along the way. While some of the tribes in the area seemed eager to trade, others were suspicious and hostile toward David's party. One group of tribesmen even fired muskets and arrows at them from close range.

The Zambesi Expedition returned to Shupanga by mid-December. On January 10, 1863, the *Pioneer* started steaming up the Zambesi with the *Lady Nyassa* in tow. After reaching the Shire River several days later, the two boats had to be pulled single file through the Shire's shallow spots.

As they continued further upriver, they found that conditions along the Shire were horrible. A number of slave parties had recently swept through the region, attacking and burning villages, taking away their food, and capturing many people as slaves. Skeletons could be seen everywhere, in the villages and along the paths. In other villages they found starving people who had lost all hope and were just waiting to die. Each day the remains of about a dozen dead people floated downriver past their boats, some of them to be eaten by crocodiles.

The opening months of 1863 brought four more deaths from illness of people associated with the Zambesi Expedition and the Universities Mission. That included the young man who had served as the expedition's mineral geologist, one of Livingstone's hired African men, and two UM missionaries.

Livingstone's company reached Mamvira, the lowest of the Murchison cataracts, on April 10. David fell seriously ill in early May. For a week he was too sick to leave his bed, but then gradually recovered throughout the remainder of the month. A few members of the expedition, including John Kirk and Charles Livingstone, received Livingstone's permission to return to England. David hated to see them go, but he was grateful for their five years of sacrificial service.

Livingstone's remaining party started preparing to transport the sections of the *Lady Nyassa* on ox-drawn carts around the Murchison Cataracts. However, at the beginning of July David received an official letter telling him that the British Government had decided to end the Zambesi Expedition. The Government appreciated all the hard work and sacrifices of Livingstone and his men, but because the expedition had not had greater success, it was thought to be too expensive and too dangerous to continue.

Once again there was not enough water in the Shire and Zambesi to take the *Pioneer* and the *Lady Nyassa* to the coast until after the rainy season returned. Heavy rains finally came in mid-January of the following year, 1864, allowing David's company at last to start downriver. Along the way they stopped at the base of Mount Morambala, a few miles north of where the Shire joined the Zambesi. Several months earlier the Universities Mission had moved its station to Mount Morambala. Subsequently the UM relocated to the island of Zanzibar, where it set up a school for children who had been rescued from slavery.

Now as David's party descended the Shire, they paused at Mount Morambala to take onboard forty-two women and children, as well as two UM missionaries who had stayed behind to safeguard them there. Those missionaries later took the widows and orphans to Cape Town where they were cared for by Christian people.

Shortly after reaching the mouth of the Zambesi River in the middle of February, the *Pioneer* and the *Lady Nyassa* were towed by two large British ships to Mozambique, up Africa's southeast coast. The *Lady Nyassa* was towed by the *Ariel*. Captain William Chapman of the *Ariel* offered to take Livingstone on his large ship, knowing it would provide a much smoother ride across the ocean. But David chose to stay with his African companions on the *Lady Nyassa*.

At one point in the voyage the vessels were caught in a hurricane. The *Ariel's* engines stalled when the thick rope towing the *Lady Nyassa* became twisted up in the big ship's propeller. The bow (front) of the *Ariel* swung around and headed straight toward the broadside of the *Lady Nyassa*. For a few moments it looked like the large ship would crash right over the smaller vessel.

'Doctor, what shall we do?' Livingstone's companions cried out in terror.

'We will wait till the final seconds,' David shouted above the howling wind and crashing waves, 'then we'll have to leap into the sea. The men of the *Ariel* will throw life ropes to us as they pass by, and we must all try to grab onto them. Then we'll be pulled to safety.'

Thankfully, however, it did not become necessary to do that. At the last minute the *Ariel* crossed just in front of the *Lady Nyassa*. Through skillful maneuvering of his ship in the rough seas, Captain Chapman swung back around, and another hawser (tow rope) was gotten to the small steamer so it could once again be pulled along.

After they reached Mozambique, the *Pioneer* was turned over to the British Navy and taken back to the Cape. Livingstone and some of his group steamed to Zanzibar in the *Lady Nyassa*. It wasn't possible to find a buyer for the steamer at Zanzibar, so David decided to take it to Bombay, India, and sell it there.

Reliable sources told him: 'It will likely take you eighteen days to travel the 2,500 miles to Bombay. You should arrive there well before the stormy monsoon season begins in late May or early June.'

David and his small crew of three British and nine African men (all of whom had been with him on the Zambesi Expedition) left Zanzibar the last day of April. Throughout the voyage they had twenty-five days when the wind and water were 'dead calm'. That greatly hampered their progress and increased the length of their voyage to forty-five days. They had fourteen tons of coal on board, enough to provide them with steam power for only four or five twenty-four-hour days, so they needed to use it sparingly.

After the monsoon season started at the end of May, huge waves thundered against the stern (rear) of the *Lady Nyassa*, making the entire vessel quiver. When at last they reached Bombay on June 13, David was full of thanks to God for protecting them through their long, perilous voyage.

After leaving the *Lady Nyassa* in the charge of a trusted acquaintance, Livingstone left Bombay for England on June 24. He reached London a month later. Just over six years had passed since he first left Britain at the beginning of the Zambesi Expedition in March 1858. Those years had been full of many hardships, heartaches and disappointments for David.

Many people would have been left full of doubt or bitterness by it all. They would have wanted nothing more to do with Africa. However, David's trust in God and his personal determination in the face of hardship were unshaken. He still desired to be used of God to bring Christianity and commerce to southern Africa, and to help put a stop to the horrific slave trade there.

Difficult Journeys and New Discoveries

While back in Britain for a little over a year, Livingstone enjoyed being able to spend some time with most of his children. He was concerned to learn that his oldest son, Robert, had sailed to the United States of America and joined the Union Army (of the northern States) to fight in that country's Civil War. Livingstone's fears for his son came about when Robert was later captured and died in a prisoner of war camp at just eighteen years of age.

Agnes was now a young woman of seventeen and had become quite tall. Thomas, age fifteen, had also grown tall, but had been in poor health for a long time due to having a kidney problem. Oswell was twelve and had been doing well in his schooling. This was David's first opportunity to meet and get acquainted with his youngest child, Anna Mary, who was already five years old.

During Livingstone's second visit to Britain he wrote another long book about his recent years of travel in Africa. This new book was all about the Zambesi

Expedition's explorations of the Zambesi, Shire and Rovuma Rivers as well as its journeys to Lake Nyassa. In the book David also reported the terrible consequences he had seen from the Portuguese and Arab slave trades in southern Africa. He clearly called on Britain to use its powerful influence to help put a stop to the slave trade in southeastern Africa, as it had already done in southwestern Africa.

Livingstone was invited by the Royal Geographical Society to return to Africa once again, this time to explore a broad system of rivers and lakes that stretched across several hundred miles of the interior region of southcentral Africa. The main geographical purpose of those explorations would be to find out if the waters of those rivers and lakes eventually fed into the Nile River or the Congo River. (The Nile River system is over 4,100 miles long and flows north, eventually emptying into the Mediterranean Sea. The Congo River system is over 2,700 miles long and flows west into the Atlantic Ocean.)

For thousands of years travelers in Africa had never been able to discover exactly where the headwaters of the Nile River began. That remained an unsolved mystery of great interest among British geographers in Livingstone's lifetime.

While David was fascinated with trying to locate the headwaters of the Nile, he still thought it was far more important to help bring Christianity and commerce to southern Africa. He wrote to a friend at this time:

'I would not agree to go simply as a geographer, but as a missionary and do geography by the way [on the side]. Because I feel I am in the path of Christian duty when trying either to spiritually enlighten these poor people, or to open their land to lawful commerce.'

As David set out on this new exploration through Africa, he wrote in his private journal: 'I mean to make this a Christian expedition, telling a little about Jesus Christ wherever we go. His love in coming down to save men will be our theme.'

Livingstone left England to return to Africa in the middle of August 1865. Upon reaching Bombay, he was able to sell the *Lady Nyassa*. After arriving at Zanzibar late in January 1866, he arranged to have a supply of beads, cloth, flour, tea, coffee and sugar sent ahead to the town of Ujiji on the east shore of Lake Tanganyika. Ujiji was the most important trading center in the inland region where David would be traveling. He sent those supplies ahead to be waiting for his use after he arrived at Ujiji.

At Bombay, Zanzibar and Mikindany Bay (a harbor north of where the Rovuma River entered the Indian Ocean), David hired around sixty men and older boys to assist him in the coming expedition. He also purchased six camels, four water buffaloes, four donkeys and two mules to use in carrying supplies. He wanted to find out if those animals could withstand the bite of the tsetse fly or if they would be harmed by it as oxen and horses were.

It took Livingstone's company four months to travel up the Rovuma River and to the eastern shore of Lake Nyassa. Many of the men became ill with fever, but quickly recovered after being treated with medicine. Sadly, however, one older boy died from his illness. The men who were in charge of the animals mistreated them, though David repeatedly and strongly protested against it. Eventually all the animals weakened and died. David could not tell if that was the result of the mistreatment or of tsetse bites.

Several of the men proved to be lazy, refusing to carry a reasonable load or to put in a regular day's march. A number of them stole food from villages and pilfered some of the expedition supplies, including gunpowder, cloth and beads.

As they neared Lake Nyassa they passed a series of large slave parties, one of which had some 1,000 captives. While making their way down around the southeastern shore of the lake, Livingstone saw the bodies of people who had been killed in a recent slave raid scattered everywhere.

Some of David's men refused to go any further than to Lake Nyassa with him. He had to send others back to the coast because of their unreliability and stealing. Of the sixty men and boys who had set out from the coast with him five months earlier, only a dozen remained with him now, eight of those being boys.

Over the course of the next six months Livingstone and his small band made their way more than 700 miles from the southern end of Lake Nyassa to the southern end of Lake Tanganyika, traveling in a northwesterly direction. They suffered a great deal of hunger, as food was in short supply due to recent Mazitu warrior forays in some of the areas through which they passed. Heavy rains began falling the second week of December, making their progress more difficult.

Two additional carriers were hired along the way to serve with Livingstone's party and did so faithfully for seven weeks. Then on January 20, 1867, they suddenly disappeared into the forest with several of David's valuable supplies. Worst of all, they made off with the entire stock of medicines. Without those David had no way of treating fevers and other illnesses.

'I was too ill with rheumatic fever to have a teaching service,' David recorded in his personal journal while stopped at a village in mid-February. 'And no medicine! But I trust in the Lord, who heals His people.' He continued to have attacks of fever in the weeks that followed.

They reached Lake Tanganyika on April 1. It had taken just three days less than one year to travel from Mikindany Bay on the coast to Tanganyika. Lake Tanganyika stretches out 418 miles north to south and is Earth's longest freshwater lake. It is also the world's second deepest lake, with a maximum depth of 4,820 feet. Lake Tanganyika had first been discovered by two other British explorers, Richard Burton and John Hanning Speke, nine years earlier, in February of 1858.

Early in May Livingstone's small band set out for Lake Moero, another sizeable body of water said to be located a considerable distance west of the southern end of Lake Tanganyika. David desired to become the first white man to visit Lake Moero and to determine whether the waters of that region flowed toward the Nile or the Congo. He then learned, however, that some Arab traders were fighting with a powerful chief named Nsama in the area to the west through which he wished to pass. So he instead traveled southwest to the village of another chief, Chitimba, where most of the Arabs were gathered.

Livingstone's party had to wait at Chitimba's village for over three months, till the end of August, while a peace agreement was worked out between the Arabs and Chief Nsama. Then David and the expedition continued slowly west, traveling with some of the Arabs who desired to trade in ivory.

Livingstone has been criticized for sometimes traveling with Arab trading parties on this and other future occasions, especially when some Arabs were known to trade for slaves. However, several important factors need to be remembered. David had always avoided traveling with Arab parties so that no one would think that he approved of their slave trading. But by this time his own band had become so small that they could no longer travel safely through some areas. There was a very real danger of being attacked by suspicious tribes which could easily plunder or kill them. In order to reach some of the regions David was supposed to explore, his band had to travel with larger Arab trading parties for their own protection.

Whenever possible, Livingstone still tried to travel only with Arab parties that were trading for ivory or other African goods rather than for slaves. He continued to speak out against slave trading to Arabs and Africans alike. In the numerous letters he was able to send now and again to friends and Government officials back in Britain, he reported the examples of slavery, its abusive treatment and sad results which he heard of and saw. Many Arab traders did not like having David travel with them, because they knew he would report to others their wicked deeds in capturing and mistreating slaves.

Livingstone's band left the Arabs they had been traveling with on November 7 and headed south toward the northeastern side of Lake Moero, which they reached the next day. Due to the difficulties and delays involved in passing through the various tribal territories, it had taken half a year to travel the ninety-three miles from the southern side of Lake Tanganyika to the northern side of Lake Moero.

Livingstone became the first white person to discover Lake Moero (modern Lake Mweru). The lake is eighty-one miles long north to south, thirty-five miles wide at its broadest point, and fairly shallow with an average depth of twenty-five feet.

After traveling along the eastern side of Lake Moero, Livingstone's party came to the village of a chief named Casembe. The village of about 1,000 people was located around fifteen miles southeast of Lake Moero. David was horrified to find that many of the villagers had been punished in the past by having their ears or hands cut off. Even some of the village's current leaders had suffered that mistreatment. David thought that Casembe's people were more savage in their treatment of each other than any other tribe he had witnessed in Africa.

It had been two long years since Livingstone had received any news from Britain. Before continuing his explorations, he wanted to make his way to the town of Ujiji on the eastern side of Lake Tanganyika for any letters and supplies that had been sent to him there. Living at Casembe's village at this time was an influential Arab trader named Mohamad bin Saleh. David described him as being 'portly' (somewhat fat), with a pleasant smile and a pure white beard. 'I will go with you back to the northern end of Lake Moero, and from there to Ujiji,' Mohamad suggested. 'It will take us only a month to reach Ujiji.'

They left Casembe's village on December 22 and arrived at the village of Kabwabwata on the northeastern side of Lake Moero the middle of January 1868. Mohamad bin Saleh's son Sheik lived at Kabwabwata. There Livingstone was informed: 'It usually takes only thirteen days to travel from Kabwabwata to Ujiji. But now during the rainy season the region between here and there is flooded. It has much mud and many swollen streams to cross. In addition, it would be hard to get canoes with which to cross Tanganyika to Ujiji at this time of year when the lake's waves are large. Many of us plan to return to Tanganyika after the rainy season ends in a few months.'

Three months later, in mid-April, Mohamad bin Saleh and others at Kabwabwata still did not intend to leave for Ujiji for another two months. Rather than continuing to wait idly at Kabwabwata, Livingstone decided to travel south to explore another large lake, Lake Bangweolo. Livingstone's party reached the lake in the middle of July. Once again, David was the first white person to visit and discover Lake Bangweolo. The modern Lake Bangweulu is forty-seven miles long and twenty-five wide, with an average depth of just twelve and a half feet.

David returned to Kabwabwata on October 22, having been away from it for six months. At last, on December 11 he was able to set out for Tanganyika and Ujiji. He could not help but realize that eleven months earlier they had been delayed at Kabwabwata because of the start of the rainy season, and now the heavy seasonal rains would soon begin again. Livingstone's band traveled with two Arab trading parties and a group of African traders from the Lake Tanganyika region.

As they trudged through the heavy rains and needed to cross many flooded streams, Livingstone developed pneumonia. For the first time in all his years of traveling, he became too weak to walk and needed to be carried on a cot-like frame called a kitanda. They reached the southwestern shore of Lake Tanganyika in mid-February 1869. One month later, after being transported in a large canoe across the lake and up its eastern shoreline, David arrived at Ujiji.

Livingstone was deeply disappointed to learn that most of the supplies he had arranged to have transported from Zanzibar to Ujiji, had never arrived. It was possible that after reaching Ujiji, they had been pilfered. For the third time in just over two years, David wrote a letter to the British Consul (government representative) at Zanzibar, asking that new supplies be sent to him at Ujiji. He also requested fifteen dependable men who could be trusted to deliver the supplies and to serve as his carriers on his future journeys.

Living among
Bloodthirsty Men

Livingstone decided he would next explore Manyuema, a large territory west of the northern half of Lake Tanganyika. Some claimed that the Manyuema tribes were cannibalistic, but others reported they were not. In recent months, for the first time ever, a few Arab parties had gone into Manyuema and had great success in trading for ivory.

David had also heard of a large river, the Lualaba, that flowed through Manyuema territory in a northward direction. He wanted to explore that river to find out if it were the western branch of the Nile River or instead led to the Congo River.

Traveling with an Arab trading party that was in search of ivory, Livingstone's band crossed Lake Tanganyika, then trekked northwest into Manyuema. On September 21, they reached Bambarre, an important Manyuema village, where some of the early Arab traders had set up their headquarters. From there the Arabs had sent out their trading parties into other parts of Manyuema.

Twice David was thwarted in reaching the Lualaba River, first by suspicious tribesmen who would not allow his band to pass through their territory, then by a month of fever and cholera that he suffered early in 1870. Cholera is a bacterial infection in the lower intestine that causes vomiting, diarrhea and dehydration.

Livingstone then heard of another Arab trader who was camped at Mamohela and who needed advice on how to cross the Lualaba River. Thinking this might be a way to achieve his own goal of reaching the Lualaba, David made his way to Mamohela. He was still quite ill and weak when he arrived, and the rainy season was underway, so he ended up staying there four and a half months. During that period, a whopping fifty-eight inches of rain fell at Mamohela.

While there David learned of two occasions in which Arab trading parties had recently attacked the Manyuema. In the first instance, nine villages were burned and forty Manyuema killed. On the second occasion, sixty goats were stolen, thirty-one people were taken as slaves and another forty Manyuema were killed.

When the leader of one of these Arab trading parties boasted to Livingstone of what they had done, David responded indignantly, 'You were sent here not to murder, but to trade.'

'No,' the man flatly contradicted him, 'we are sent to murder.'

Late in June Livingstone set out again to try and reach the Lualaba River. Only three of his faithful companions were willing to accompany him. The other members of his small band refused to go with him, fearing they would be killed.

David's progress was soon stopped by three large sores that formed on his feet. Before, when foot sores developed while traveling, he cared for them, and they soon healed up. Now, though, he had no medicine so the sores spread and became worse. David referred to these sores as 'irritable eating ulcers'. They ate away at the skin, muscle and bone of his feet! The ulcers were extremely painful, and he could walk only with the greatest difficulty.

He was forced to return to Mamohela then to Bambarre, which he reached on July 22. There he was confined to a hut for eighty days. It took more than two months for his foot sores to begin healing. Then he suffered three weeks of fever and cholera, which took away his strength and his voice for a time. Livingstone's illness on this occasion was part of a widespread cholera epidemic that swept across that part of Africa clear to the east coast. About thirty slaves died from the disease at Bambarre during that time.

While detained at Bambarre, David continued to be troubled by hearing of one instance after another when the Manyuema were guilty of bloodshed against each other. David recorded in his private journal: 'The Manyuema are the most bloody, callous savages I know.

One puts a scarlet feather from a parrot's tail on the ground, and challenges those near to stick it in the hair. He who does so must kill a man or woman!'

Early in February 1871, such senseless bloodshed struck very close to Livingstone when one of his own men, James, was killed by an arrow. Someone hiding in the forest shot James when he and others from the expedition passed by on their way to buy food.

Finally, on February 4, ten men who had been sent by the British Consul at Zanzibar to assist Livingstone arrived at Bambarre. Twelve days later, after nearly seven months of being halted at Bambarre, David was at last able to leave it. Traveling first to the southwest then to the northwest, they reached Nyangwe, an important marketplace town on the east bank of the Lualaba River, on the final day of March. Two Arab trading parties were there and had sent their people to trade with tribes on the west side of the Lualaba.

As many as 3,000 people, mainly women, gathered at the Nyangwe marketplace every few days to trade their food, clay pots, baskets and many other items. At Nyangwe the Lualaba River was some 3,000 yards across. The river was nine feet deep at its steep banks and deepened to twenty feet in the middle. Its strong current flowed north at the rate of about two miles per hour.

Livingstone's ten new carriers were afraid to go any further into Manyuema and wanted to return to the coast. They began spreading the rumor that Livingstone intended to buy a canoe in order to carry out war on the western side of the Lualaba. 'He does not want slaves or ivory,' they claimed, 'but a canoe in order to kill Manyuema.' Some members of the Arab trading parties helped to spread that falsehood. Consequently, for three and a half long months, David was unable to purchase a canoe. Any available canoes were sold instead to the Arab traders.

Many members of the Arab parties were themselves slaves who served their Arab masters on these trading expeditions. Some of those slaves were given considerable authority by their masters to carry out trade for them. Late in June, one such slave named Manilla crossed to the west side of the Lualaba River and entered into a trading agreement with the leaders of the Bagenya villages there.

This made some of the freemen (non-slaves) in the Arab trading parties very angry. 'Manilla is a slave,' they fumed. 'How dare he make an agreement with chiefs who should only be friends with freemen like us? We need to make an example of Manilla and teach the Bagenya that they must deal only with us. We will teach them all a lesson.'

As a result, on the morning of Saturday, July 15, they began attacking and burning the Bagenya villages, capturing some people as slaves and killing others. That day and the next they destroyed twenty-seven villages, murdered twenty-five people and captured forty-four women as slaves.

That same Saturday morning Livingstone, in Nyangwe, was surprised to suddenly hear rifle shots from the western side of the Lualaba. When he walked up to the marketplace, he found about 1,500 people there. He was further surprised to see three men from one of the Arab trading parties there with their rifles, as guns were usually not allowed in the marketplace. One of David's men went up and told the three armed men that they should not have their rifles there.

The day was stiflingly hot, so David started to leave the marketplace to return to his hut. When he had walked only about thirty yards outside the marketplace, he heard two rifles fired in the middle of the crowd. People threw down their wares in confusion and rushed away in panic.

As the three men opened fire on the people near the upper end of the marketplace, another group of Arab traders down by a nearby creek started shooting at the men and women who were fleeing to their canoes there. Fifty or more canoes were jammed into the small creek that led to the Lualaba, and most of them could not be gotten out in the terror and chaos that was taking place.

Many Africans left their canoes behind, leaped into the Lualaba, and started swimming toward the closest island nearly a mile away. But in doing so they were swimming against the strong current. For a time, a long line of heads could be seen of people trying to escape across the river. But most of them eventually disappeared under the water. Some of them managed to swim back to the river's edge and escape. One canoe launched out onto the river and was able to rescue twenty-one people.

David watched in horror and disbelief as the Arabs shot and killed people, and as many others drowned in the river. Of the awful things he had seen and heard, he wrote in his journal later that day, 'It gave me the impression of being in Hell.' The Arabs estimated that between 330 and 400 people lost their lives on that occasion.

Livingstone sent several men with the British flag to rescue some of the Manyuema fugitives. Without being under the protection of the British flag, David's men might have been killed. About thirty Manyuema were brought to Livingstone and stayed overnight near his house. The next day these thirty individuals were returned to their family members and friends. The head of one of the Arab trading parties told Livingstone he would do all he could to have all the Bagenya captives freed and returned to their families.

Delivered by a
Good Samaritan

'I can no longer stay in the company of Arab traders who are capable of such heinous bloodshed,' David concluded. 'I will return to Ujiji with only my small band of men, though doing so will place us in great danger along the way.'

He was chagrined at needing to turn back now. 'I only need to travel 100 miles further west to complete my exploration of the rivers and lakes of this region. Then I would know if they lead to the Nile or the Congo.'

A heavy, frustrated sigh escaped his lips as he brooded further. 'But without dependable carriers or a canoe to use, I now must return well over 300 miles to Ujiji. Including all the twists and turns in the paths along the way, it will likely be closer to 600 miles back to Ujiji. And once there I will need to wait many months for reliable carriers to be sent from Zanzibar. Only then will I be able to return and finish my explorations.'

Livingstone's band started back to Ujiji on July 20, five days after the Nyangwe massacre. Early in August they passed several villages that had recently been attacked by an Arab slave party. The local tribesmen viewed David's party as likely enemies and accosted them. One group of villagers threw stones at them. At another spot trees had been felled across the narrow forest path to block their progress. They expected to be ambushed while getting past the blockade, but thankfully no one attacked them there.

As they continued along, a large spear suddenly sailed over Livingstone's back, narrowly missing it as he crouched down. Another spear slammed into the ground barely a foot in front of him. Tragically, two members of Livingstone's party were killed in the assault. Their attackers immediately fled into the dense forest. David's men fired their guns into the forest but with no effect as nothing could be seen there.

They came to a clearing in the forest where Livingstone saw a 'gigantic, partly-rotted tree' standing on top of a twenty-foot-high mound. Fire had been set around the base of the tree. Suddenly David heard a loud crack and saw the tree falling straight toward him. He ran back a few steps, and the tree thundered to the ground one yard behind him, breaking into several sections and covering him with dust.

The other men who had scattered in all directions to get out of the way of the falling tree, came running back to him, shouting: 'Peace! Peace! You will finish all your work in spite of these people and in spite of everything!' David, too, took this as a sign that the Lord would give him success in carrying out his plans.

Throughout the final two months of the journey back to Ujiji, Livingstone suffered much illness and weakness. Of the final part of the trek he later reported: 'I felt as if dying on my feet. Almost every step was in pain.'

A single simple sentence that David penned in his personal journal on October 3 of the current journey is extremely significant: 'I read the whole Bible through four times while I was in Manyuema.'

Livingstone had faced many painful trials and deep discouragements while living among the Arab traders and the Manyuema tribesmen. During those two years he read through the entire Bible four times, or on average seven chapters of Scripture every day! No doubt God greatly used His Word, the Bible, to provide David with a steady stream of encouragement, reassurance, guidance and renewed strength, thus helping him to get through the many difficulties.

David reached Ujiji on October 23. In response to the earlier letters he sent to the British Consul at Zanzibar, new supplies had been delivered to him at Ujiji. But now on his first evening back at Ujiji, he was distressed to learn that the man who had been placed in charge of his belongings, had sold all of them. Three thousand yards of Livingstone's cloth and 700 pounds of his beads had been traded away in exchange for food, drink and other goods for the unfaithful steward and his associates.

David now found himself with almost no food or possessions in Ujiji. Referring to Jesus's parable of the Good Samaritan in Luke 10:30-37, David later wrote: 'I felt, in my destitution, as if I were the man who went down from Jerusalem to Jericho, and fell among thieves. But I could not hope for priest, Levite or Good Samaritan to come by on either side.' Then, however, he added: 'But when my spirits were at their lowest ebb, the Good Samaritan was close at hand.'

Late in the morning of November 10, the sound of rifles being fired from the top of the hill some 500 yards east of Ujiji was suddenly heard in the town below. At first the townspeople feared that Ujiji was under attack. But the group of people at the top of the hill carried a flag at the front of their procession, approached the town slowly, and fired their guns only to signal their approach, all of which showed that they were a peaceful caravan and not an attacking war party. Soon hundreds of townspeople ran up the hill to welcome the approaching caravan.

From the covered porch of his house beside the Ujiji marketplace, Livingstone watched the excitement caused by the caravan. 'Rejoice, old master,' men soon called out to him, 'it is a white man's caravan. It may belong to a friend of yours.'

Minutes later the Arab leaders in Ujiji gathered at Livingstone's house and said, 'Come, arise, friend David. Let us go and meet this white stranger. He may be a relative of yours. If God is pleased, he is sure to be a friend. The praise be to God for His goodness!'

They reached the center of the marketplace just moments before the caravan did. The American flag at the head of the procession told the nationality of the caravan's leader. The leader, a young man of thirty years of age, pressed through the dense crowds and slowly walked toward Livingstone and the semicircle of Arabs who stood behind him. A hush fell over the large crowd of more than 1,000 people who eagerly desired to see and hear what was about to happen.

The American wore a new flannel suit which he had reserved for this special occasion. The evening before his boots had been polished and his pith helmet freshly chalked in preparation for this meeting. He observed that Livingstone was pale, looked tired and had a gray beard. He wore a dark blue cap, like what a sea captain would wear, with a faded gold band around it. He had on a red waistcoat and a pair of gray tweed pants. Livingstone's clothes were clean but showed signs of patching.

At five feet, five inches tall, the American was three inches shorter than David. Approaching Livingstone in a dignified fashion, he took off his hat, bowed, and asked, 'Doctor Livingstone, I presume?'

'Yes,' Livingstone replied simply with a kind smile, lifting his cap slightly in respectful greeting to the young man.

'I thank God, Doctor,' the American announced aloud, 'I have been permitted to see you.'

'I feel most thankful that I am here to welcome you,' David responded sincerely.

The American was Henry Morton Stanley, a traveling newspaper correspondent of the *New York Herald*. Stanley had been sent out by the *Herald* to find out if Livingstone were still alive and, if so, to assist him in any way he could.

While David was deep in the interior of Africa in recent years, there had been periodic rumors that he had died. Both in Britain and in America there was considerable interest in learning if Livingstone were still living and what new discoveries he was making. The proprietor of the *New York Herald* knew that considerable acclaim would come to his newspaper if it were the first to discover and publish this information. That is why he sent Stanley out in search of Doctor Livingstone.

David had been eating only two small, tasteless meals a day before Stanley's arrival at Ujiji. But now he ate four delicious and nutritious meals each day with the food that Stanley provided for him. 'You have brought me new life,' David kept telling his generous new companion.

Stanley also brought Livingstone the first news he had heard from the outside world in over two years, as well as the only personal letters he had received from family and friends during that time. Stanley delivered a whole bag of mail which the British Consul at Zanzibar had sent for him.

The *New York Herald* reporter had arrived in Zanzibar in January of that year, 1871. There he collected six tons of equipment and supplies for his upcoming expedition to find Livingstone. He hired 191 people to serve as his carriers, armed guards and cooks. He also purchased twenty-seven donkeys to carry supplies and two horses for riding.

Stanley's expedition first traveled for three months to the Arab settlement of Unyanyembe, which was 400 miles inland from the coast. Unyanyembe was located on the main Arab trade route between the coast and Ujiji. Stanley had to wait there for three months because a powerful African chief was blocking the route between Unyanyembe and Ujiji, some 200 miles further west. Stanley left Unyanyembe with a smaller company of fifty-four well-armed men on September 20, skirted around the area blocked by the African chief, and arrived at Ujiji on November 10.

Livingstone quickly regained his strength and health following Stanley's arrival. Then the two men, accompanied by twenty Africans to assist them, took a four-week, 300-mile roundtrip by canoe to the northern end of Lake Tanganyika and back to Ujiji. They were the first white men ever to visit the northern end of the lake and discovered that the rivers at that end of Tanganyika flowed into rather than out of the lake. Before that many had wondered if the waters of Lake Tanganyika flowed out of its northern end and helped feed the Nile River. Livingstone and Stanley determined that was not the case.

During this journey some of their possessions were stolen while they slept beside the lake one night, and they were confronted with suspicion at other villages. Past mistreatment by Arab traders and a recent war between two area tribes had left the region unsettled. Some thought Livingstone's party were marauders who had come to attack them.

One afternoon they entered a small cove in front of a village that appeared to be peaceful toward them and prepared to spend the night. David and two of his African companions went on a walk to see the nearby landscape. When they arrived back at the hill overlooking their campsite, they spotted an angry mob of local tribesmen gathering at the beach. Seven or eight of David's party had taken refuge behind their canoe and were half pointing their rifles at the threatening crowd. Stanley, wearing his revolver belt, was standing outside his tent, keeping an eye on the tense situation.

A naked young tribesman, thoroughly drunk and barely able to stand on his feet, was beating the ground with his loincloth while shouting angrily. The young man's father, the local chief, was just as drunk though not as violent in his behavior. David approached the two men and calmly asked, 'My friends, what is the matter?'

He learned that they had an unresolved conflict with the Arabs and had mistaken his party as being an Arab band. Rolling up the sleeve of his shirt and revealing his untanned arm, Livingstone said: 'Look at my arm.

You see how white my skin is. I am a white man, an Englishman. My skin is not dark like an Arab's.'

He then sat down, saying, 'Come sit with me. Let's talk quietly together. I and all my men come in peace. I have a gift for you.' The chief and his son joined him in sitting down. Livingstone asked one of his associates to bring some cloth and beads and offered them to the two men. He continued speaking to them in a gentle manner, like a patient father talking with his children.

Gradually their loud protests against the cruel treatment they had experienced from the Arabs began to subside. But suddenly the old chief jumped up and began pacing back and forth excitedly. He then slashed his own leg with the blade of his spear and cried out, 'Look how my enemies have wounded me!' Apparently he meant to dramatically show the white man the type of harm his enemies had brought to him and his people.

When the chief did this, half his people who had gathered with him fled from the beach. But one old woman began loudly scolding him, saying: 'You must want to get us all killed! You need to quiet down and accept the gift the white man is willing to give you.' Other women joined her in similarly correcting their chief. In the end, the incident ended peacefully. The chief and his son went away quietly, feeling pleased with the gifts they had received.

Faithful to the End of Life

After Livingstone and Stanley returned to Ujiji in the middle of December, the newspaper man sometimes asked David about his future plans. When David spoke of finishing his explorations in Africa, Stanley suggested: 'But your family, Doctor, they would like to see you, oh so much! Let me tempt you to go home to Britain with me. All you have to do is hint to me any material needs you have, and they will be met. Let the search for the sources of the Nile wait for now. Come home and rest. Then, after a year's rest and restored health, you can return and finish what you have to do here.'

However, Livingstone's response was always the same: 'No. Of course I would like to see my family very much, but I must not go home yet. I must do my duty and finish the task I have set out to do. I believe this is what my family and friends would want me to do. It is only my lack of supplies and dependable men that has prevented me from discovering the sources of the Nile by this time. If I had only been able to go one month further west from the Lualaba River, I could have said, "The work is done."'

Seeing that he was not going to change Livingstone's mind, Stanley made a different suggestion: 'Then, Doctor, let me escort you to Unyanyembe, where some of the goods sent to you from Zanzibar are still waiting for you. I also left behind there a large supply of cloth and beads, guns and ammunition, cooking utensils, clothing, boats, tents and other items. I will give these to you, to use in finishing your explorations. While you rest in a comfortable house at Unyanyembe, I will hurry down to the coast and organize a new expedition made up of fifty or sixty reliable, well-armed men. I will send them back to you with other possessions to help you be more comfortable on your journeys.'

Livingstone agreed to this plan. He, Stanley and their African assistants left Ujiji the final week of December. The rainy season had begun, and heavy rains fell on them nearly every day throughout their journey to Unyanyembe.

A month after leaving Ujiji, they were suddenly attacked by a huge swarm of wild bees. David at first rolled on the ground, trying to get some of the insects off himself. He then dashed into a bush and tore off a branch. He waved the branch around his head as he continued trying to run away from the bees. Their whole group ran along for about half a mile, with the men behaving as wildly as the pack animals, as all of them were stung repeatedly.

Stanley was extremely concerned about Livingstone on this occasion. In the days before the attack, David's boots had become so worn out that his feet were blistered and bleeding. When the bees attacked, they settled in handfuls in David's hair and stung him many times on his head and face.

To make matters worse, their party had a long march of eighteen miles to complete that day. Stanley sent four men with a kitanda (cot) to carry David. 'But,' the newspaper man reported, 'the stout old hero refused to be carried and walked all the way to camp. After having a cup of warm tea and some food, he was as cheerful as if he had never traveled a mile.'

They reached Unyanyembe on February 18, 1872. Once again it was found that many of the supplies that had been delivered to Unyanyembe for Livingstone had been stolen. Some of the goods that Stanley had left behind were also missing, but he had so many possessions he was able to give David far more than had been stolen from him.

Stanley left Unyanembe to travel back to the coast on March 14. He had been with Livingstone for four months and four days. As it turned out, Stanley was the only white person David saw during his final seven years of exploring in Africa.

After reaching Zanzibar on May 7, Stanley kept his promise to Livingstone in hiring fifty-seven men to assist him in carrying out his final explorations. Stanley sent those men back to David at Unyanyembe together with abundant additional supplies to aid him in his future journeys. The men and supplies reached him at Unyanyembe on August 14, five months to the day after Stanley had left Livingstone.

David and his new party of carriers left Unyanyembe on August 25. They made their way to the southern end of Lake Tanganyika and from there continued south and west toward Lake Bangweolo. Early in January 1873, after the rainy season had begun, they entered a broad floodplain region that stretched out for many miles in all directions. The area had many flooded rivers, streams and marshes that needed to be crossed. They reached the northeast shore of Lake Bangweolo by the middle of February.

Just after midnight on February 17 the village at which Livingstone's company was staying experienced a 'furious attack' of red driver ants. The ants swarmed into David's tent and onto his feet, biting fiercely. As soon as he fled outside the tent, he was covered with ants, making him look like a person with a heavy rash from chicken pox or measles. For an hour or two David's companions helped to pick ants off his arms and legs. Then they led him to a hut where he was able to rest for a while, until the ants invaded and drove him from it as well.

Grass fires were lit to drive off the ants, and hot ashes were poured on the insects. Then a steady rain began to pour and continued until noon. The ants did not leave the village and the area until late that afternoon.

Livingstone's company was unable to travel along the northern shore of Lake Bangweolo due to tribal fighting and a lack of food in the region to the west. In March and April, David's party instead made their way slowly along the eastern and southern sides of the lake. Throughout the remainder of the rainy season, which lasted through the first full week of April, the plains along the sides of the lake continued to be flooded.

For several weeks David had been losing much blood from bleeding hemorrhoids. The constant bleeding left him so weak that he had to be carried across the swollen streams and flooded plains. He had also been riding a donkey. But after he became too weak to walk or ride, his companions started carrying him a short distance each day on a kitanda.

On Tuesday, April 29, they reached Ilala, the village of a chief named Chitambo. Livingstone was placed in a hut on a bed that was made of a large pile of sticks covered with a thick layer of grass. One of the supply boxes was placed near his bed to serve as a table. His medicine chest, a cup and a candle were placed on it. A boy in the party, Majwara, slept inside David's hut, to assist him if needed.

Late Wednesday evening, around midnight, Livingstone had Susi, one of his faithful African companions for many years, pour a cup of hot water for him and leave it on the bedside table. Sometime after Susi went to his own hut, David managed to get out of his bed and to kneel beside it. His upper body stretched forward across the bed, and he placed his head in his hands on the pillow.

It seems likely, as many people have suggested, that David made the effort to get up and kneel beside his bed in order to pray. It is not known what he prayed about that night, but God his loving heavenly Father no doubt heard his prayers and cared for him in his final moments of earthly life.

As Majwara went to sleep that night he saw Livingstone kneeling beside his bed and a candle burning on the bedstand. When the boy woke up some time later, Livingstone was still kneeling in the exact same position, and the candle had burned down quite low. Majwara hurried to Susi's hut nearby and called out: 'Susi, come see the Master. I am afraid. I don't know if he is alive.'

Susi, Majwara and four other of Livingstone's men went to David's hut and found that he was dead. David Livingstone had died early that Thursday morning, on May 1, 1873. He was sixty years old at the time of his death. His spirit went immediately to live in Heaven with his Savior Jesus Christ, whom David had faithfully and tirelessly served for so many years.

Livingstone's men firmly decided that they must return his body to the coast of Africa, so it could be taken from there to his homeland to be buried. After burying his heart and other internal organs nearby Chitambo's village of Ilala, they carefully prepared and wrapped his body so it could be safely and discreetly transported. They then carried his remains through a challenging journey of some nine months and around 1,000 miles to the coast, which they reached in mid-February 1874.

From there Livingstone's body was taken by ship to Zanzibar then back to England, where it arrived in London in the middle of April. That Saturday, April 18, David Livingstone received the highest honor from his country, that he could in death, by being buried in Westminster Abbey. That is where many other prominent people from throughout Britain's history have been buried.

Livingstone's noble desires for Africa — to have Christianity and commerce brought to southcentral and southeastern Africa, and to have the slave trade ended in that portion of the continent — began to be dramatically fulfilled within a few short months and years after his death:

For many years Livingstone had written in his letters, government reports and books about slavery practices in southern Africa. His writings made British people aware of the African slave trade and its devastating consequences. What he reported played a major role in British citizens and their political leaders finally deciding that the evil slave trade must be stopped throughout southern Africa.

Though this news did not reach David before his death, in the final months of his life the British Government began putting strong pressure on the

Government of Zanzibar to help bring an end to the East Africa slave trade. As a result, beginning on May 1, 1873, *the very day Livingstone died*, the British Navy put a stop to slaves being shipped from the coastal ports of southeastern Africa. Just five weeks later the great slave market in Zanzibar was permanently closed. Less than two years after that, all movement of slaves by land (not just by sea) was also outlawed, thus bringing an end to the slave trade throughout all southern Africa.

Within five years of Livingstone's death a pair of British commercial companies established twelve trading stations and three large plantations stretching from the mouth of the Zambesi River up to Lake Nyassa, and from there across to Lake Tanganyika. This greatly promoted fair and healthy trade practices in those areas.

Starting two years after Livingstone's death and continuing for the next thirteen years, six different missionary societies started missionary works at Lake Nyassa, in the Shire highlands, at Lake Tanganyika, at Rovuma River, at Zanzibar, and in the regions of Tanzania, Uganda and Congo. Thus, David Livingstone's highest desire was fulfilled as well: Christianity and the Christian Gospel were spread throughout southcentral and southeastern Africa.

David Livingstone's Journeys, 1841-1856

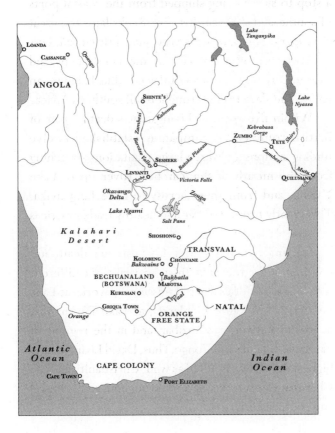

David Livingstone Timeline

1813   David Livingstone is born in Blantyre, Scotland, on March 19.

1823   David begins work in a cotton factory and night school classes at age ten.

1832   David becomes a Christian.

1834   David dedicates his life to be a missionary.

1838   David begins his London Missionary Society training in Chipping Ongar, England.

1840   David finishes his medical training in London and leaves to be a missionary in Africa.

1841-   David carries out three ministry journeys to the
1843   Bechuana tribes north of Kuruman.

1843   David Livingstone and Rogers Edwards establish the Mabotsa mission station.

1845   David marries Mary Moffat at Kuruman (January 2), establishes the Chonuane mission station.

1847   Mission station moves from Chonuane to Kolobeng.

1848   Chief Sechele becomes a Christian.

1849   David crosses the Kalahari Desert and discovers Lake Ngami with William Oswell and Mungo Murray.

1850   David and his family return to Lake Ngami.

1851   David and his family reach the Makololo. Livingstone discovers the upper Zambesi River

1852   Mary and the Livingstone children return to Britain.

1853-   David's journey to Loanda on the west coast.
1854

1854-   David's transcontinental journey to Quilimane on
1856   the east coast. Livingstone discovers Victoria Falls along the way (November 1855).

1857　David's first visit home to Britain. He writes *Missionary Travels and Researches in South Africa*.

1858　David leads the Zambesi Expedition.

1859　David explores the Shire River and discovers Lake Shirwa and Lake Ngami. David's family returns to the U.K.

1860　David returns with the Makololo to Chief Sekeletu.

1861　David explores Lake Ngami.

1862　Mary Livingstone rejoins David in Africa on February 1 but dies on April 27. David explores the Rovuma River.

1863　David's final journey up the Shire River. The British Government recalls the Zambesi Expedition.

1864　David's perilous sea voyages to Mozambique and Bombay, India. David's second visit home to Britain.

1865　David writes *Narrative of an Expedition to the Zambesi and Its Tributaries*. He returns to Bombay en route back to Africa.

1866-
1867　David's journey to Lake Nyassa (reached August 1866) and Lake Tanganyika (reached April 1867).

1867　David discovers Lake Moero (November).

1868　David discovers Lake Bangweolo (July).

1869-
1871　David's journeys in Manyuema. He witnesses the massacre at Nyangwe (July 15, 1871).

1871　Henry Morton Stanley delivers David from destitution at Ujiji.

1872　Livingstone and Stanley travel to Unyanyembe. David travels back to Lake Bangweolo.

1873　David dies at the village of Ilala on the south side of Lake Bangweolo on May 1.

1874　David's body is transported to England and buried in Westminster Abbey in London, April 18.

Thinking Further Topics

Chapter 1: Cotton Mill Work and Night School Studies

From the time he was just ten years old, David Livingstone needed to work long hours in a cotton mill and attend school at night. How might God have used those challenges to prepare David for the hardships he would experience as a missionary?

Chapter 2: Becoming a Christian and a Missionary

What did David realize and do at age nineteen that resolved the inner spiritual struggles he had had for several years? How do John 3:16, Romans 6:23 and Ephesians 2:8-9 teach that we do (and do not) come to have God's gifts of salvation and eternal life?

Chapter 3: First Ministry Journeys in Africa

How did David and his Christian companions help the young orphan girl who was going to be sold against her will? What does James 1:27 teach about Christians helping orphans, widows and others who are in distress?

Chapter 4: Attacked by a Lion

Name some positive characteristics of Mary Moffat that attracted David to her? Why is it important for young adult Christians to exercise wisdom in deciding whom they will marry?

Chapter 5: Leading a Chief to Faith in Christ

David had ministered to Sechele and his people for nearly three years before the chief (but no one else) became a Christian. How does that encourage us in our own efforts to lead others to saving faith in Jesus?

Chapter 6: Challenging Journeys Far Further North

While David was pleased to discover Lake Ngami, what was he even more enthused about learning from that journey? David had to make three long, difficult journeys before he was able to reach the Makololo tribe. What does his example teach us about persevering for God?

Chapter 7: Traveling among Friends and Foes

What were two significant sacrifices that David and Mary needed to make as he was seeking to minister to the Makololo? What are some of the sacrifices that Christian families today may need to make? How does God provide for and protect those who serve him today?

Chapter 8: Trekking across the Continent

Rather than returning to his family, David thought it was his duty to lead his Makololo men safely back to inner Africa. What can we learn from his example? David wrote: 'The end of the geographical feat is but the beginning of the missionary enterprise.' What does this statement show his highest priority was?

Chapter 9: Leading the Zambesi Expedition

In agreeing to lead the Zambesi Expedition, what were some of the ways in which David hoped to bring greater good to many more people in Africa? How did David respond when he realized the Zambesi River could not be used as a waterway to inland Africa? How should we respond when we seem to encounter a barrier to our plans?

Chapter 10: New Explorations and Fulfilling a Promise

God rescued David from a charging rhinoceros and from a dangerous whirlpool in the river. Has God ever rescued you or someone you know from great danger or death? How does God rescue us from spiritual danger and death? (Romans 6:23; 1 Corinthians 10:13).

Chapter 11: Interfering with the Slave Trade

When David and his companions interfered with the slave trade, they accomplished some good but also faced some opposition. What are some ways we can take a stand against what is clearly wrong? What should we do or say if some people oppose us for doing so?

Chapter 12: Sad Deaths and Destruction

David was extremely sad when Mary died, even though he knew she had gone to Heaven. How do the responses of Jesus, Mary and Martha to the death of Lazarus show that it is natural to be sad when someone we love dies? (John 11:17-36; see also 1 Thessalonians 4:13-18).

Chapter 13: Difficult Journeys and New Discoveries

When David returned to Africa, what continued to be a higher priority to him than geographical exploration and discovery? How can we, like David, properly balance serving God with carrying out the other responsibilities and activities of life?

Chapter 14: Living among Bloodthirsty Men

While traveling in Manyuema for two years, David spoke against several instances of terrible bloodshed carried out by Arab slave traders. What does the Bible teach about such bloodshed? (Proverbs 1:10-19; 6:16-18).

Chapter 15: Delivered by a Good Samaritan

David spoke of Henry Morton Stanley as being the Good Samaritan who came to his rescue. According to Christ's parable of the Good Samaritan in Luke 10:29-37, who is our neighbor for whom we should be a Good Samaritan?

Chapter 16: Faithful to the End of Life

What might David have prayed about as he knelt at his bedside shortly before he died? How does it encourage us to know that God hears our prayers and knows our needs even if no one else does? David's greatest dreams and desires for Africa were brought about by God beginning in the months and years immediately after his death. How does that encourage us to remain hopeful and faith-filled in our service for the Lord, even if we do not yet see the desired results? (1 Corinthians 15:58; Galatians 6:9).

Fact Files

Arabs, Portuguese and British in Southern Africa

For more than a thousand years before David Livingstone arrived in Africa, Arabs had traded along the southeastern coast of Africa. They mainly traded for slaves, ivory and gold dust, which tribes from the interior of Africa brought to them at the coast. By Livingstone's time the Arabs also carried out trade in inland Africa north of the Zambesi River.

During the 1400s and 1500s Portuguese explorers sailed along Africa's coastlines, and the Portuguese set up their rule over Angola (southwestern Africa) and Mozambique (southeastern Africa). They established a few forts along about 250 miles of the southern reaches of the Zambesi River in an effort to control the ivory and slave trade carried out in that region. However, in Livingstone's time the Portuguese struggled to maintain control over the area, and even needed to pay heavy financial tribute to powerful tribes in the vicinity to maintain peace with them.

Britain initially was one of several European nations that participated in the west African slave trade during the 1700s. Britain played the key role in putting a stop to the slave trade in southwestern Africa beginning in the 1830s and in southeastern Africa beginning in the 1870s. Britain took permanent control of

Cape Colony in south Africa in 1806, to prevent France from interfering with the shipping and trade interests of the British East India Company. Because of Portugal's control in name only over the southern Zambesi River region, Livingstone thought that Britain and other nations should be permitted to carry out legitimate trade (but not slave trade) throughout the Zambesi area.

Ivory Trade

For centuries the ivory tusks of elephants and rhinoceroses were a valuable trade commodity for Africans with Europeans. The ivory and slave trades often went hand-in-hand, as captured slaves were used to carry heavy tusks from the interior of Africa to the coast, where both were sold. So many elephants and rhinos were killed for their tusks in the 1800s and early 1900s that their numbers were drastically reduced, causing them to become endangered species. Most African countries now prohibit or greatly limit hunting of them. But demand for ivory remains relatively high, leading to poaching and the ongoing endangerment of these animals.

Livingstone's Legacy in Africa Today

In recent years a Pew Foundation research study reported that sixty-three percent of Sub-Saharan Africa is identifiably Christian. The highest percentages of Christians are in Congo, Uganda, Malawi, Tanzania, and

Kenya, which are all territories indirectly influenced by David Livingstone or in which he traveled and ministered. To this day Livingstone continues to be admired and appreciated throughout southern Africa for his life of sacrificial service for the spiritual and temporal good of the African people.

OTHER BOOKS IN THE
TRAIL BLAZERS SERIES

William Carey, Expecting Great Things
ISBN 978-1-5271-0793-9
Thomas Clarkson: The Giant with one Idea
ISBN 978-1-5271-0677-2
Thomas Cranmer, The King's Ambassador
ISBN: 978-1-5271-0877-6
Elisabeth Elliot: Do the Next Thing
ISBN: 978-1-5271-0161-6
Jim Elliot: He is no Fool
ISBN 978-1-5271-0465-5
Olaudah Equiano, A Man of Many Names
ISBN 978-1-5271-0876-9
Betty Greene: Courage has wings
ISBN 978-1-5271-0008-4
Martin Luther, Reformation Fire
ISBN 978-1-78191-521-9
Polycarp: Faithful unto Death
ISBN 978-1-5271-1029-8
Samuel Rutherford: The Law, the Prince and the Scribe
ISBN 978-1-5271-0309-2
Francis & Edith Schaeffer: Taking on the World
ISBN 978-5271-0300-9
Charles Simeon, For Christ in Cambridge
978-1-5271-0841-7
Elaine Townsend, At Home Around the World
ISBN 978-1-5271-0732-8
Jack Turner, Truth in the Arctic
ISBN 978-1-5271-0792-2

For a full list of Trail Blazers, please see our website:
www.christianfocus.com
All Trail Blazers are available as e-books

CHRISTIAN FOCUS PUBLICATIONS

Christian Focus   Christian Heritage   CF4K   Mentor

Christian Focus Publications publishes books for adults and children under its four main imprints: Christian Focus, CF4K, Mentor and Christian Heritage. Our books reflect our conviction that God's Word is reliable and Jesus is the way to know him, and live for ever with him.

Our children's publication list covers pre-school to early teens. We also publish personal and family devotional titles, biographies and inspirational stories that children will love.

From pre-school board books to teenage apologetics, we have it covered!

**Find us at our web page:
www.christianfocus.com**

CF4•K
Because you're never
too young to know Jesus